# THE ESSENTIAL

# INTERIOR DESIGN HANDBOOK

# THE ESSENTIAL

# INTERIOR DESIGN HANDBOOK

**Edition One**

# CONTENTS

# Introduction



# #1 - Essentials



# #2 - Areas



# #3 - The Finer Details



# Conclusion

# INTRODUCTION

## *What Is Interior Design / Interior Architect / Spatial Design?*

We spend over 90 percentage (%) of our day in interior spaces. Despite this, most people take interior spaces for granted, barely noticing the furniture, colour, textures and other exciting elements - let alone the form of the space itself. Sometimes, of course, the design of an interior is meant to catch our attention. Maybe it's the excitement of a casino, the panelling of a high-end restaurant, or the soothing backdrop of a relaxing spa facility.

As you are reading through this handbook, you must have an interest in interior design. It might be you have always enjoyed rearranging the furniture in your home. Maybe you like to draw indicative floor plans for your home. It could be a relative or friend is within the construction industry, and you may be involved in the construction of a building in some way. Perhaps you saw a program on television or online, and it has inspired you to learn more about the profession of interior design.

The interior design profession is more than what is portrayed on social media and television. Educators and professionals have defined the profession of interior design over the years. This widely accepted definition provides help to understand what the profession is all about.

Interior design is a multi-faceted profession, which creative and technical solutions are applied within a structure to achieve a beautiful built interior space. These solutions are functional; they enhance the quality of life of the user, and are aesthetically attractive. These designs are created in response to and coordinated with the builds shell and acknowledge the location and social context of the project. Designs must adhere to code and regulatory requirements and encourage the principles of environmental sustainability. The interior design process follows a systematic and coordinated methodology, including research, analysis and integration of knowledge into the creative process, whereby the needs and resources of the client are satisfied to produce an interior space that fulfils the goal of the project.

# INTERIOR DESIGNER vs INTERIOR DECORATOR

Interior designers are not Interior decorators, and in turn, Interior decorators are not interior designers, even though the general public usually does not see the distinction between the two.

"Interior design is not the same as decoration."

Decoration is the redecorating or furnishings of a space with fashionable or decorative items and materials. Decoration, although an important and effective element of an interior space, it is not concerned with human interaction or human behaviour. Interior design is about human behaviour, human interaction, discovery and enhancing the user's experience of a space.

Despite the fact an interior designer might offer interior decoration services, an interior decorator does not have the education and experience to perform many of the roles and services of a professional interior designer. A decorator is essentially concerned with the aesthetic decoration of the interior and rarely has the expertise, for example, to provide the necessary drawings for the construction that are routinely produced by a professional interior designer.

# WHAT IS IT THAT INTERIOR DESIGNERS DO?

Interior design professionals provide the client with functionally successful and aesthetically attractive interior spaces. An interior designer might specialise in working with private residences or with commercial interiors such as hotels, hospitals, retail stores or offices. In many ways, the interior design profession benefits society by focusing on how space's and interior environments should look and function.

A professional interior designer uses their education and training to consider how the design impacts the health, safety, and welfare of the occupant. Many projects today consist of careful consideration of sustainable design in the selection of furniture and materials used inside the interior. Planning the arrangement of walls, selection of furnishings, and specifying aesthetic embellishments for the space are all tasks the designer uses to bring the interior to life. A set of useful and aesthetic requirements expressed by the client becomes a reality.

While designing a domestic home or a large commercial interior space, the interior designer will care out multiple tasks using an array of skills and knowledge, gained throughout their education and professional life within the field of design. The interior designer must take into account building and safety regulations, deal with environmental concerns, understand mechanical systems, and basic construction of buildings.

They must have the ability to communicate design concepts through hand sketches, scaled drawings and other documents used within the industry. Another important responsibility involves how to control all tasks that must be carried out to complete a project, from a large 1000-room casino-hotel or as small as a one-bedroom studio apartment. Furthermore, the interior designer must have the business skills to complete projects within budget for the client while making a profit. Of course, the interior designer selects colours, materials, and products so that what is supposed to occur within the spaces can be achieved.

# #1 Essentials

Managing an interior design project requires a great deal of creative understanding as much as the design itself, and the best projects begin with a carefully planned project schedule. Usually, the project process is broken down into specific phases to establish decision-making milestones, both with the design team and the client. At the beginning of the design phase, endless options present themselves. Still, as the design progresses, the number of options progressively reduces as the project gathers speed around specific themes and configurations.

Drawings are the primary format through which a designer will communicate their design to the client and contractors. The mode of drawing changes as the project is defined and finessed. At the beginning of concept design, freehand sketches are the best way to test your designs. In contrast, later in the process, computer-aided design (CAD) is necessary to finalise dimensional decisions and coordinate with third-party consultants. New technologies are making it easier to explore design concepts in three dimensions at several stages of the design process.

## CHAPTER ONE

# STARTING YOUR INTERIOR PROJECT

The notion of beginning an interior project can be scary; however, with a little strategic planning, a project can be started easily and effectively. Irrespective of the size of the project, four basic stages have to be considered from the start: project site, program, schedule, and budget. Those four stages are not often determined solely through the client or the designer, but generally by both in collaboration within the first initial meetings. The fewer uncertainties, the smoother the process becomes.

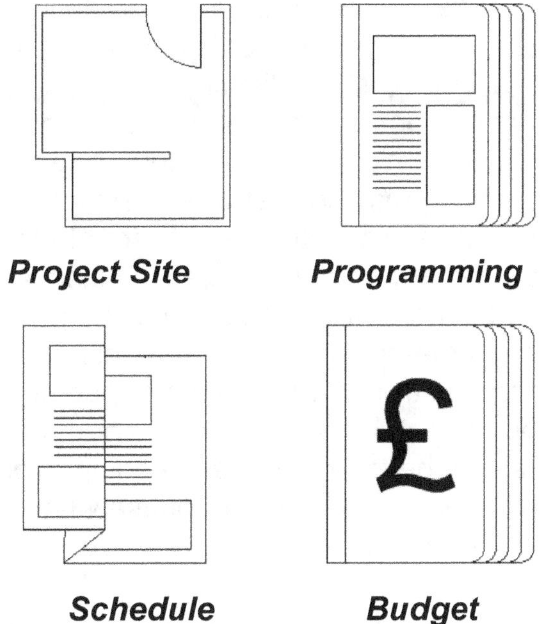


## PROJECT SITE

In general, a client engages an interior designer when a site or space is selected. It is then the designer's responsibility to review the space to make sure that it'll meet the client's desires (set out within a brief). Occasionally, a client may additionally have a few site options that the designer will test to check which one best fits the client's needs. Each of these routes suggests the client is working towards a particular program; but, sometimes, the physical space generates the program naturally. In this situation, the designer's challenge is to decide the best layout for the space and design a program within those parameters.

## PROGRAMMING

Programming is the process of defining the wishes of those who will use the space in advance of creating the design. Whether or not for a small home bathroom renovation or a newly constructed restaurant, this exercise should evaluate the functional performance, opportunities, and limitations of the existing space. Furthermore, the program must show what spaces, features, or attributes must introduce to enhance the functionality and give an appropriate and compelling enhancement to a space. The programmatic goals needs to be precisely drafted within a brief, the document that outlines all functional, dimensional, and relational requirements. This list of goals will shape the basis for evaluating design solutions in subsequent phases of the project.

The process of programming is broken down into three essential types of activities: gathering, analysing, and documenting information. The method of establishing the project goals and the format of the program can range massively. For smaller projects, collecting data and studying the client's needs are even more vital; producing a written document is less so in some situations. To avoid miscommunication with your client, a record of the process need to be made. Thus, programming may consist of a single questionnaire, a comprehensive interview, or a list that explains the issues. Together with the number and types of luggage, shoes, long or short dresses/suits within a wardrobe, or the amount of cupboard space needed to accommodate dishes, fine china or counter-top appliances. For larger commercial/ corporate projects, the designer will need to listen and put in order criteria from a wide range of people. Frequently, the interior designer has to incorporate conflicting information and make suggestions to the client that can have implications beyond physical planning. Documentation is essential. In all instances, the designer is required to prioritise wish lists to make meaningful and countless design decisions.

| Gathering Information | Analyzing Information | Documenting Information |
|---|---|---|
| Collect floor plans from client | Analyze interview notes | Document client's mission and project goals |
| Visit and walk the site while taking photos | Create diagrams of ideal spatial relationships | Summarise program for current and future growth |
| Report field observations | Determine staff counts | Include meeting notes |
| Client structure and end users<br>-Who makes the decisions?<br>-Who uses the spaces? | Develop lists of type and numbers of spaces. | Obtain client approval on program and projections |
| Compile information on client | Define specific needs within a given space | Compile report |

Even though this step might sometimes appear unnecessary, programming is crucial to the design process due to the fact it is here that the client identifies their problems and desires. Appropriate communication is key to articulating the program and managing expectations for the design phase. A lack of understanding of the goals at this stage might also result in cost overruns during the construction phase or, even more unfavourable, a project that does not meet the client's fundamental needs. Preferably, the program serves as a map from which design objectives, spatial selections, and building constraints are elaborated.

# SCHEDULE

The preferred project schedule specifies not only the interior designer's responsibilities, but also the crucial choices to be made by way of the client, in addition to the vital role of the contractor as a member of the project team. As a result, the schedule should address all the project milestones, in the form of an organized checklist, and assign to a team member the first duty for oversight. Programs consist of, but are not restricted to, establishing time-frames for completing contracts and acquiring existing site surveys. Defining the length of a design phase; reviewing concept designs and budget sign-off; bidding and negotiating with contractors; obtaining permits; defining construction length; and securing handover dates. If the date for handover is already secured, it is best to work backwards from this date to determine the length of each milestone. Reviewing the general time-frame against the checklist of activities will determine its reasonableness. It is also crucial to research the duration of the regulatory and approval processes in the local area, due to the fact they regularly consume extra time than initially anticipated.

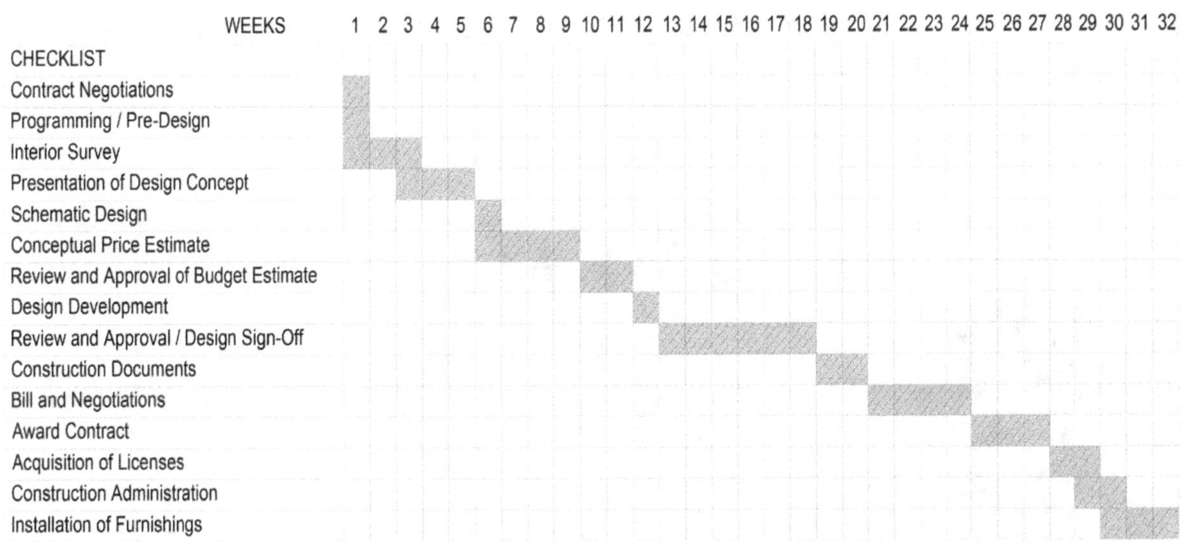


*The above table is a typical schedule of works for a medium-sized restaurant which dictates all steps from initial client introductions through to completion of the project.*

# BUDGET

Creating a project budget is essential for streamlining the design process. It immediately reveals the scope of work and the extent of the finish. Budgets for a project get divided into two categories, hard and soft costs. For an interior design project, hard costs will cover the construction and fixtures, furnishings, and equipment (FF&E). An average amount for an FF&E budget is 10 percentage (%) of the general construction cost. Soft costs include, however, are not limited to, consultant's costs, interior designer's fees, project control fees, licensing fees, insurance, and project contingencies.

A designer's number one concern is to meet the budget for hard costs. To sure that a budget is realistic, a conceptual pricing estimate should be carried out early in the process. For smaller projects, its usually not practical and cost-effective to have a quantity surveyor (QS) or contractor on board from the beginning, Instead, the designer may be able to offer a "ballpark" figure primarily based on their past experiences. The danger is that construction costs can be extremely volatile and subject to change depending on many elements, including inflation and shifting marketplace conditions. So for early pricing studies or ballpark expectation, it is vital to encompass contingencies for unknown elements. There are several forms of contingencies, whose percentages of the total estimate will change as the design develops.

### Design Contingencies

Money reserved for elements within the design usually not identified during a pricing study. The earlier a pricing estimate is formed, the higher the percentage for design contingencies have to be. As the design is defined, this percentage decreases until it disappears at the end of the construction phase. These contingencies range from 5 to 10 percentage (%) of the overall construction estimate.

### Construction Contingencies

Money reserved for unknown situations because of the renovation of existing sites. Those contingencies can range from 5 to 15 percentage (%) of the general estimate.

### Escalation

Money reserved for increased prices for materials and labour due to time lapses from the preliminary pricing study to actual production. These contingencies can range from 3 to 5 percentage (%) per year, from when the project was initially priced.

### Change Order

Documents that are submitted by a contractor indicating a change in the price, schedule, or service to complete the project.

### Competitive Bid

Open request to bid on a project based on completed construction drawings and specifications, the job is typically awarded to the lowest bidder.

### Invitation to Bid

Request pre-qualified contractors from a pre-determined list to bid on a project based on completed construction drawings and specifications.

### Value Engineering (VE)

Efforts to reduce project costs by eliminating or downgrading details that add costs without benefiting a particular function or answering the program requirements, VE requires the involvement of the client, contractor, and designer.

# SCOPE OF A PROJECT

As the design for a small project is further developed, it is essential to work with the selected contractor who will estimate the project costs based on drawings and specifications that the designer provides. For small projects, estimates are typically not based on square meter-age, but rather, should identify and price all construction materials and labour costs. For medium to large projects, either a quantity surveyor (QS) or a construction manager will prepare the budget. Quantity Surveyors (QS) are hired exclusively to put together construction estimates. Construction managers are contractors/builders that are hired early in the design process to manage the cost of a project through the design phases. These experts typically have significant market experience and can establish a project budget based on a pound (£) or Dollar ($) value per square meter; however, the budget should always be tested against a detailed breakdown based on the project scope. For substantial projects, it is standard to request several estimates to test the market value of the project. Price variations are more symptomatic of different material quantities than of varying unit prices, and the quantity surveyor can help resolve these disputes.

# BUDGET FORMATS

For smaller design projects, budgets are generally itemised based on how a general contractor would ask a sub-contractor to bid on the design project. The trades get broken down into general categories which include carpentry, plumbing, electrical, plaster and paint, mill-work, and so forth. For medium to large projects, budgets are formatted according to the Construction Specification Institute's (CSI) index, the standard breaks down construction costs by trade, helping the designer examine where most of the construction costs are concentrated. The table below outlines the CSI index and expands on the divisions, which can be most relevant to an interior design project.

| Index | Area | Sub-Area | |
|---|---|---|---|
| 1000 | General Notes | | |
| 2000 | Site Works | | |
| 3000 | Masonry | | |
| 4000 | Concrete | | |
| 5000 | Metal | 5100 | Metal Materials |
| | | 5200 | Metal Finishes |
| | | 5300 | Decorative Metal |
| 6000 | Plastic and Wood | 6100 | Carpentry Finishes |
| | | 6200 | Architectural Woodwork |
| | | 6300 | Plastic Finishes |
| 7000 | Thermal and Moisture | | |
| 8000 | Windows and Doors | 8100 | Metal - Doors and Frames |
| | | 8200 | Wood - Doors and Frames |
| | | 8300 | Plastic - Doors |
| | | 8400 | Door and Frame Hardware |
| | | 8500 | Entrance and Shopfronts |
| | | 8600 | Metal - Windows |
| | | 8700 | Wood - Windows |
| | | 8800 | Plastic - Windows |
| | | 8900 | Glazing |
| 9000 | Finishes | 9100 | Plaster |
| | | 9150 | Metal Supports |
| | | 9200 | Aggregate |
| | | 9250 | Tile |
| | | 9300 | Terrazzo |

| | | 8800 | Plastic Windows |
|---|---|---|---|
| | | 8900 | Glazing |
| 9000 | *Finishes* | 9100 | Plaster |
| | | 9150 | Metal Supports |
| | | 9200 | Aggregate |
| | | 9250 | Tile |
| | | 9300 | Terrazzo |
| | | 9350 | Acoustic Treatments |
| | | 9400 | Special Finishes |
| | | 9450 | Wood Flooring |
| | | 9500 | Stone Flooring |
| | | 9550 | Masonry Flooring |
| | | 9600 | Tactile Flooring |
| | | 9650 | Carpet |
| | | 9700 | Special Flooring |
| | | 9750 | Floor Treatment |
| | | 9800 | Special Coating |
| | | 9850 | Paint |
| | | 9900 | Wall Covering |
| 10000 | *Specialties* | 10100 | Chalkboards |
| | | 10200 | Wall Guards |
| | | 10300 | Lockers |
| | | 10400 | Partitions |
| | | 10500 | Storage Shelving |
| | | 10600 | Toilet and Bath Accessories |
| | | 10700 | Wardrobes and Closets |
| 11000 | *Equipment* | | |
| 12000 | *Furnishings* | 12100 | Fabrics |
| | | 12200 | Manufactured mill-work |
| | | 12300 | Window Treatments |
| | | 12400 | Furniture |
| | | 12500 | Rugs and Mats |
| | | 12600 | Multiple Seating |
| | | 12700 | Planting and Planters |
| | | 12800 | Artwork and Statues |
| 13000 | *Special Construction* | | |
| 14000 | *Mechanical* | | |
| 15000 | *Electrical* | 15100 | Lighting |
| | | 15200 | Communications |
| | | 15300 | Controls |

CHAPTER TWO

# PROJECT MANAGEMENT

The interior designer and client must attain a common understanding of the contract, fees, and design process for a project to be successful. On larger projects, a project manager will assume responsibility for coordinating these aspects of the job. For smaller projects, the interior designer has both to design and manage the project. Management issues accrue during the beginning of a project, and they must be addressed throughout the project to ensure the fees, schedules, and agreements are all met.

## CONTRACTS

Step one in beginning a new project is for the interior designer and client to finalise and sign a contract. The contract will define the scope, qualifications, assumptions, exclusions, duration, and terms of the project. Ideally, it is set up to separate the scope into precise design tasks, for example, the number of meetings and when they are held, the number of flights covered by the client (for international projects) or the number of renderings or sample boards to be produced. When forming a comprehensive scope, the contract needs to include a list of qualifications, which are limitations placed on the scope. A typical qualification will be for example "the project fee is based on 4,550 square meters" or "the project design fee is based on an eight-month duration". Including a list of assumptions will avoid miscommunication; for instance, "as-built/ surveyed AutoCAD drawings will be provided by the client" or "the project will be phased into two design and construction projects". It is equally important to list exclusions in the contract, consisting of "an interior survey is not within the contract" or "fixtures selections are not part of the contract." These will assist in identifying issues or specialists needed for which the designer is not responsible. The contract must also provide a written description or a visual schedule that outlines the project timeline.

# TERMS OF AGREEMENT TO INCLUDE IN EVERY CONTRACT

Payment terms
Payment Details
Code interpretations
Ownership of documents
Limitations of liability
Termination or suspension
Insurance and indemnification
No consequential damages
Your standard Terms and Conditions

## MISTAKES TO AVOID WHEN ESTABLISHING A CONTRACT

Not defining a scope of works
Starting before the contract is signed
Not red-flagging additional services as they arise
Not listing reimbursable items
Not halting work when payments are overdue
Not defining a method of compensation.

# DESIGN FEES

When negotiating a design fee, it is up to the designer and the client to agree on
the fee structure. For most design sectors, there is no such thing as a "typical"
or "standard" fee for design services, due to the different nature of individual
projects. A private residential project, for instance, can range from a small single
room renovation to a new six-bedroom dwelling with multiple out-houses, and
the fee may be best structured on an hourly basis. On the other hand, for a large
commercial project, it would be reasonable to assume a fee based on the number
of square meters (or feet). That being said, most interior designers choose between
several methods of structuring fees, either alone or in combination, and adjust them
to fit a client's particular needs.

# TYPES OF FEE STRUCTURES

### Fixed Fee (or Flat Fee)
A sum that is based on human resources, hourly rates, and duration of services, expenses are eliminated from the fixed fee.

### Hourly Fee (or Time and Material)
They are paid for every hour spent by the designer on a project, based on a predetermined hourly rate. In addition to the hourly fee, materials (colour copies, printing, samples) are also billed.

### Cost Plus
Fee-based on the designer purchasing furniture, materials, and services (carpentry, drapery, picture framing), and resell to the client at the designer's price, plus an additional specified percentage to compensate the designer for their time.

### Percentage of Construction Costs
Fee structured on the overall cost of the construction budget.

### Calculated Area Fee
Fee determined by multiplying the projects area, generally in square meters, by an agreed-upon cost per square meter. Typically, the larger the project, lower the cost per square meter.

It is now commonplace for interior designers to charge an hourly fee for design services and cost-plus for products. Usually, an interior designer will request a retainer in advance. A retainer is money paid directly by the client to start the design process. Better known as an Engagement fee, it is usually due while the contracts are being signed and is then deducted from the project's final invoice.

## ENGAGING CONSULTANTS
Hiring a consultant will depend on the scale, type, and scope of a project. For example, however, essential lighting is within a kitchen, it may not be necessary to contact a lighting specialist, but their experience is crucial for an art gallery or hospital. It is the designer's responsibility to make recommendations to the client for hiring consultants. The chart below lists the specialists, an interior designer and architect may recommend to the client for a project.

| Consultant (Third Party) | Interior Designer | Architect | Responsibilities |
|---|---|---|---|
| *Acoustic Engineer* | O | O | Design, detail, and specify construction methods for acoustic applications. |
| *Art Consultant* | O | | Recommend and install artworks. |
| *Color Specialist* | O | O | Recommend and specify paint scheme. |
| *Fire Protection Engineer* | O | O | Design fire sprinkler system and provide calculations for building officials. |
| *Furniture Consultant* | O | O | Recommend, select, and specify furniture, fixtures, and equipment. |
| *Kitchen Consultant* | O | | Design and detail of custom kitchens. |
| *Landscape Architect* | | O | Design ground plane and landscape components. |
| *Lighting Consultant* | O | O | Design and specify lighting and lighting controls. |
| *Mechanical, Electrical, and Plumbing Engineers* | O | O | Design and specify mechanical, electrical, and plumbing systems. |
| *Media Consultant* | O | | Design and install audio-visual systems. |
| *Signage/Wayfinding Consultant* | O | O | Design and specify building signage. |
| *Sustainability Consultant* | O | O | Provide recommendations for integrating sustainable solutions. |
| *Structural Engineer* | O | O | Design and specify structural components of the project. |

# DESIGN PHASES

All consultants must address the standard phases of the design process. On the next page shows the duration and goals for each phase for a small-to-medium-sized interior design project. Depending on the circumstances of a project, the timeline can vary massively; however, the project goals should be adhered to for each design phase.

# PROJECT PHASES DEFINED

**Programming**: Identity, evaluation, and documentation of the client's needs and desires in a written document. These can become the basis for evaluating design solutions in future phases.

**Conceptual Design:** The brainstorming phase of the design process, where many options and concepts are taken into consideration, evaluated and discussed. The overall aim here is to obtain client approval for a single design concept so one can be further developed as the project progresses, and to agree on a direction for the style and aesthetic intent of the project.

**Design Development:** This is the most design-intensive phase of the design project, in which all design elements are developed, along with the wall partitions and furniture layout; wall, window, floor, and ceiling finishes; furniture, fixtures, and mill-work; colour, finishes, and hardware; and lighting, electrical, and communication systems. The goal is to outline and obtain the approval of all the design suggestions.

**Construction Documents:** Development of working drawings and specifications that define the approved design for non-structural interior construction, materials, finishes, equipment, furnishings, and fixtures. At the end of this specific phase, the designer communicates the design intent in an illustrated and written format for construction purposes.

**Construction Administration:** Acting on behalf of the client as their agent, the designer must approve all shop drawings and conduct regular site visits throughout the construction phase, to ensure that the project is built according to the designer's documents. This is usually done by-weekly with the client, followed by a meeting to discuss any changes and upcoming milestones.

*Below is a indicative program for a small to medium sized project - 3500ft2*

# PROGRAMMING

### *2 Weeks*
- Negotiate a contract
- Create a project schedule
-Survey and document the existing site
-Determine the design objectives and requirements
- Document the project goals
- Confirm any consultants that may be needed

## CONCEPTUAL DESIGN
### *3 Weeks*
- Prepare illustrations to describe each design concept
- Review the concepts with the client
- Identify safety and building code issues
- Evaluate and confirm a design to be developed

## DESIGN DEVELOPMENT
### *6 Weeks*
- Develop the approved designs
- Prepare drawings, plans, elevations and details
- Develop art, accessory and signage schedules
- Appoint an estimator/ quantity surveyor to price the design

## CONSTRUCTION DOCUMENTS
### *8 Weeks*
- Obtain client approval of scope of works based on pricing
- Prepare documents to start construction
- Prepare specifications
- Tender drawing packages to qualified contractors
- Help the client with awarding contracts

## CONSTRUCTION ADMINISTRATION
### *Length of on-site construction*
- Confirm building permits have been issued
- Review and approve shop drawings and samples
- Visit the site throughout construction
- Oversee installation of FF&E
- Prepare a snagging list of pending construction issues

## CHAPTER THREE

# DRAWING BASICS

The ability to draw is essential to the design process. In the interior design world, the meaning "to draw" takes many forms. It can refer to hand sketches, to computer-aided drawing, or even to photography and other methods of communication. Many techniques have been established to ease the transmission of visual data and ideas about a design, and it is essential to understand how they function within the world of the interior designer.

## MEASUREMENT IN INTERIOR DESIGN

Before the pen hits the paper, an interior designer must learn the language of measurement. The worldwide system of measurement referred to as the international system of units, its the most widely used standard for determining the length, weight, and or volume of an item and its relation to other objects. It combines a decimal system whose the base unit is a meter, which when increased or reduced by way of a power of 10, generates all other units of measure. Designers working within the United Kingdom should be familiar with the metric system and the U.S. customary units system. Derived from a method firstly developed inside the U.K., the latter is an irregular system that combines numerous unrelated measurements - inches and feet, as an example - for linear measurement.

## CONVERTING UNITS OF MEASURE

Often, dimensional units are interchanged easily, but it is useful to know a way to change between units. Designers will discover a series of articles and websites with a lot of conversion tables for length, area, and volume, amongst other measurement types. Many online calculators will allow for quick conversions of specific dimensions. Interior designers will most frequently turn to the following formulas.

| Multiply | by | resulting |
| --- | --- | --- |
| | | |
| inches | 25.4 | Milimeters |
| feet | 304.8 | Milimeters |
| feet | 0.304.8 | Meters |
| yards | 914.4 | Milimeters |
| yards | 0.914 | Meters |

| Multiply | by | resulting |
| --- | --- | --- |
| | | |
| Milimeters | 0.039.370 | inches |
| Milimeters | 0.003.281 | feet |
| Meters | 3.280.8 | feet |
| Milimeters | 0.001.093.6 | yards |
| Meters | 1.093.613.3 | yards |

# LINEAR CONVERSIONS

| Inches | | Milimeters (mm) | | Centermeters (cm) | | Meters (m) |
|---|---|---|---|---|---|---|
| | | | | | | |
| 0.25 | | 6.35 | | 0.635 | | 0.00635 |
| 0.5 | | 12.7 | | 1.27 | | 0.0127 |
| 0.75 | | 19.1 | | 1.91 | | 0.0191 |
| 1 | | 25.4 | | 2.54 | | 0.0254 |
| 1.25 | | 31.8 | | 3.18 | | 0.032 |
| 1.5 | | 38.1 | | 3.81 | | 0.038 |
| 1.75 | | 44.5 | | 4.45 | | 0.045 |
| 2 | | 50.8 | | 5.08 | | 0.051 |
| 3 | | 76.2 | | 7.62 | | 0.076 |
| 4 | | 101.6 | | 10.16 | | 0.102 |
| 5 | | 127 | | 12.7 | | 0.127 |
| 6 | | 152.4 | | 15.24 | | 0.152 |
| 7 | | 177.8 | | 17.78 | | 0.178 |
| 8 | | 203.2 | | 20.32 | | 0.203 |
| 9 | | 228.6 | | 22.86 | | 0.229 |
| 10 | | 254 | | 25.4 | | 0.254 |
| 20 | | 508 | | 50.8 | | 0.508 |
| 30 | | 762 | | 76.2 | | 0.762 |
| 40 | | 1,016 | | 101.6 | | 1.016 |
| 50 | | 1,270 | | 127 | | 1.270' |

# UNDERSTANDING DRAWING CONVENTIONS

For legibility and comprehension, designers will use several graphical conventions in their drawings that speak the designs equally to clients, consultants, and contractors. In a critical abstraction, lines, symbols, and text all integrate to bring the designer's vision for the project.

# LINE WEIGHTS AND TYPES

Lines are crucial to speak the language of an interior designer. Lines convey a project's proposed plan, reveal the sectional quality of the space, and visually cue the reader to topics of importance, type, and purpose. Line weights and classes may be created through various media, each manually and digitally.

## Dashed Lines

Line types have many functions in a drawing package. The designer determines the relative meaning for specific weights; however, heavier lines are generally reserved for plans and section cuts, at the same time lighter lines form the outlines of surfaces and furniture within a room.

— — — — — Dashed x5

— · — · — · — · — · — Dash - Dot - Dash

– – – – – – – – Dashed

**Medium to Light**

———— 0.05mm

———— 0.09mm

———— 0.15mm

**Heavy**

———— 0.20mm - Partitions

———— 0.30mm - Inner Walls

———— 0.50mm - Secondary Structure

———— 0.60mm - Structure

Dashed lines represent many unique elements, from items which are hidden from view to items above (shelves above a bathroom counter), from the form of wall partitions to changes in level. They can also be tied to representative trades, for instance, to reveal structural grids, electric wiring, lighting and switching, or mechanical routing.

Ranking of objects in a plan drawing is established through the careful use of line weights and types. Below, the walls that are cut are the heavily rendered; furniture and built-in furniture are lighter, and hidden elements such as shelving and cabinetry are shown with dashed lines.

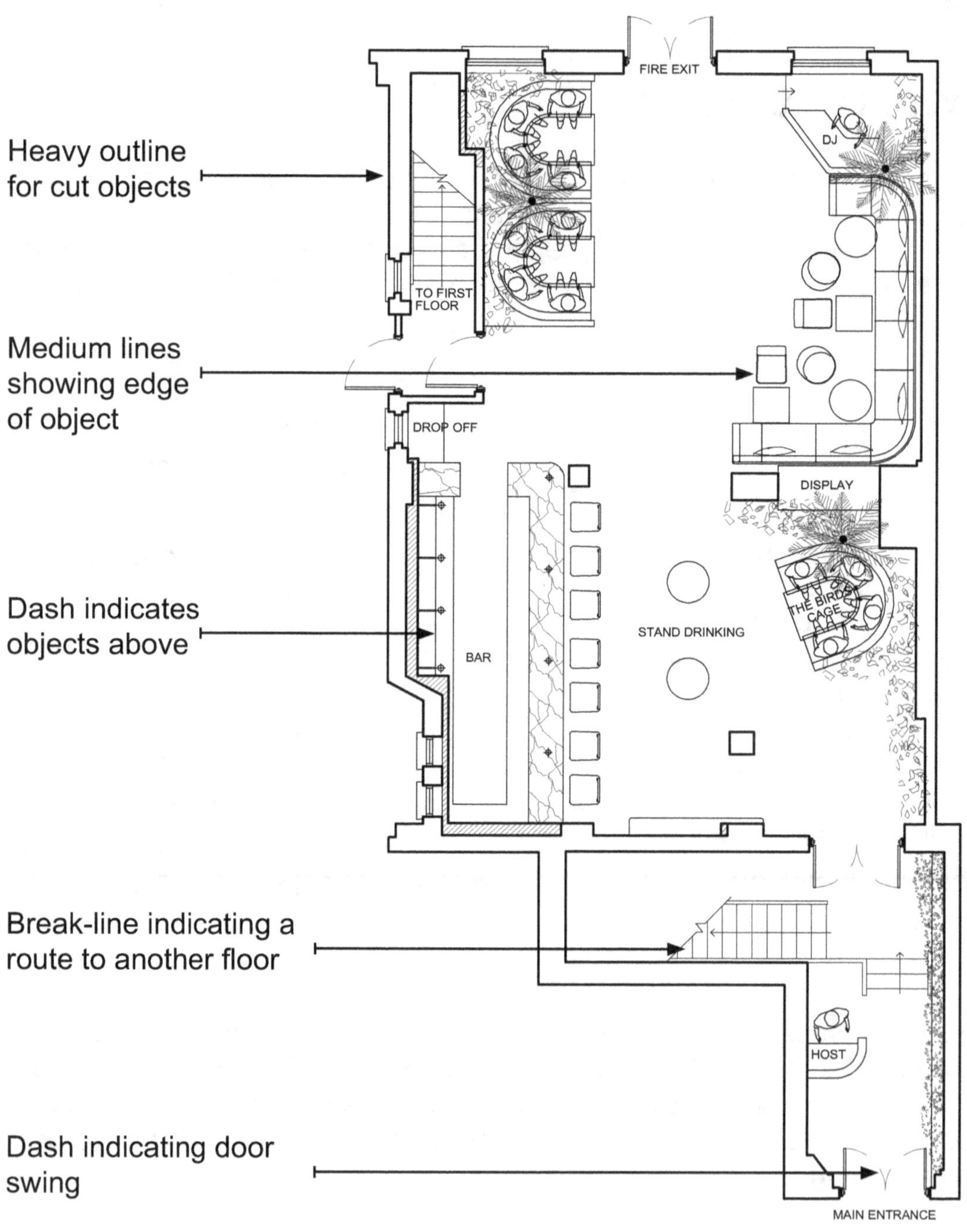

# DRAWING SYMBOLS

Drawing symbols provide a comprehensive language via which to specify the essential elements in drawings throughout the drawing package. Below are some of the symbols generally used for an interior drawing package.

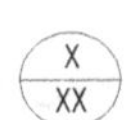

***Drawing indicator***: Gives a tag to each specific drawing of a sheet.

***Wall or Detail section***: Indicates on a plan drawing where a corresponding drawing is cut through.

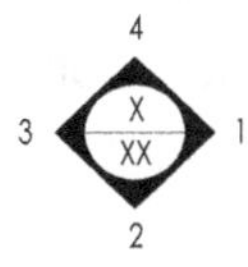

***Interior elevation***: Placed within the center of a plan, showing the direction of sections / elevations.

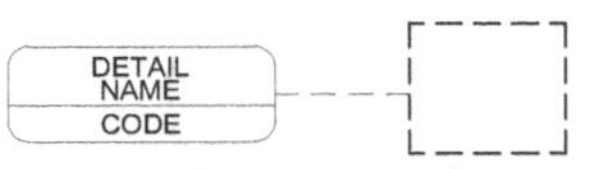

***Enlarged detail call-out***: Will highlight a specific part of a plan / drawing to a corresponding enlarged detail.

***N, E, S, W Sign***: Placed on a plan to indicate the direction of a compass bearing.

***Drawing Label***: Placed at the bottom left of each drawing to give it a specific drawing title and scale.

***Break-Line***: They are used to remove part of a drawing, and also to shorten objects which have the same shape throughout their length.

***Revision Cloud:*** A revision cloud is used for reviewing or redlining items to indicate the parts of the drawing that need to be updated or annotated. The letter dictates the issue.

**Window Type**: The number identifies the window type or the glass type, placed next to every different type.

**Door Type**: The number identifies the door type or the fire-rating type, placed next to every different type.

**Wall Type**: The number identifies the wall type/ detail of each section of wall.

**Centreline**: Used when an item needs to be centered to a space, no need to add dimensions.

**Room Tag**: Added to each room on a plan to indicate the room type and corresponding code.

**Wall Covering**: The number identifies the wall covering type to be used on each wall. (Wallpaper)

**Floor Covering**: The number identifies the flooring material and type to be used.

**Wall Finishes**: The number identifies the wall finish type to be used on each wall. (hard finish like marble)

**Wall Lighting**: The code identifies the sconce type to be used on each wall. Referenced back to a schedule.

**Ceiling Lighting**: The code identifies the pendant type to be used on each wall. Referenced back to a schedule.

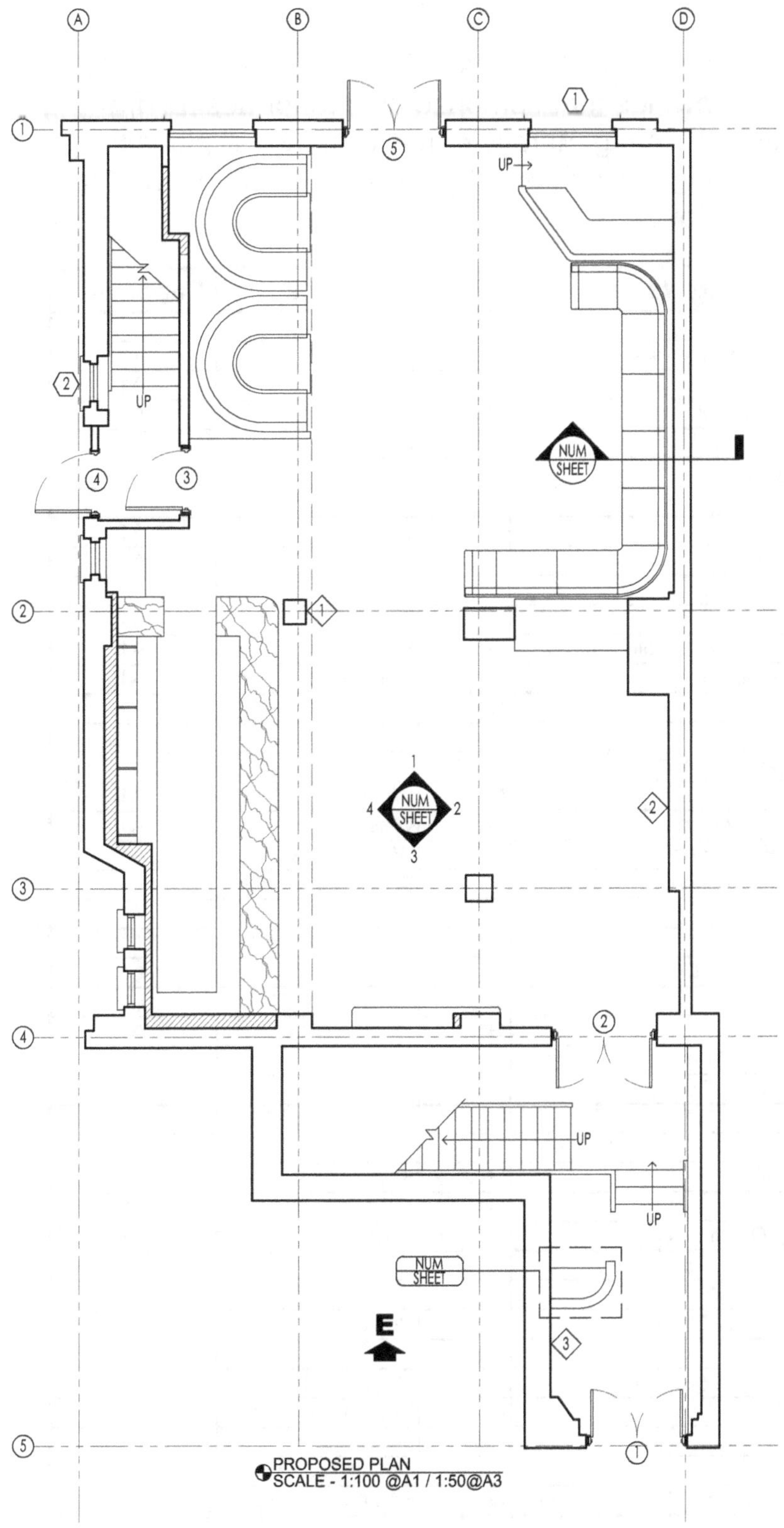



Symbols, tags and notes on a plan drawing are typically keyed to different drawings inside the interior package, including but not limited to reflected ceiling plans, elevations, sections, and details. Elements needed to enforce a design are easily read from drawing to drawing, and revisions are easily coordinated. Dimensions are indicated in strings throughout the plan, or a few instances, inside the plan itself. Legibility of textual content and numbers are essential to read a plan easily. A clean to read text like 'ARIAL' would be best for these items.

# DRAWING ORDER

The order of drawings may vary from one design studio to another. For clarity and organization, the types of drawings that comprise an interior design drawing package are numbered in sections that generally move from overall plans to specific details. After these drawings, consultants' drawings should follow in a sequence similar to that listed below.

| Drawing Code | Drawing Name | Floor | Area | Paper Size |
|---|---|---|---|---|
| Plans | | | | |
| GA.G.00 | General Arrangement Plan | G | All Areas | A1 |
| GA.G.01 | Furniture Layout | G | All Areas | A1 |
| GA.G.03 | Low Level Electrical | G | All Areas | A1 |
| GA.G.04 | High Level Electrical | G | All Areas | A1 |
| GA.G.05 | Flooring Layout | G | All Areas | A1 |
| Elevations | | | | |
| EL.01.01 | Front Elevation | G | External | A1 |
| EL.02.01 | Interior Sections | G | Internal | A1 |
| Joinery | | | | |
| JD.G.01 | Front Bar Detail | G | Bar | A1 |
| JD.G.02 | Low Level Back Bar Detail | G | Bar | A1 |
| JD.G.03 | Rear Privacy Screen | G | Restaurant | A1 |
| JD.G.04 | Wine Wall | G | Bar | A1 |
| | | | | |
| Washroom Details | | | | |
| WD.G.00 | Male WC Elevations | G | Washrooms | A1 |
| WD.G.01 | Female WC Elevations | G | Washrooms | A1 |
| WD.G.02 | Unisex WC Elevations | G | Washrooms | A1 |
| WD.G.03 | Corridor WC Elevations | G | Washrooms | A1 |
| | | | | |
| Doors | | | | |
| D.G.01 | Lobby to Resturant Door | G | | A1 |
| D.G.02 | DDA Door | G | | A1 |
| D.G.03 | Rear Exit Door | G | | A1 |
| D.G.04 | BOH Door to Kitchen | G | | A1 |
| D.G.05 | Washroom Lobby Door | G | | A1 |
| | | | | |
| Architectural Details | | | | |
| AR.G.01 | Canopy Detail | G | Kitchen | A1 |
| AR.G.02 | Canopy Detail | G | Kitchen | A1 |
| AR.G.03 | Drop Ceiling Detail by bar | G | Restaurant | A1 |
| | | | | |
| Flooring | | | | |
| FL.G.01 | Herringbone Fade Detail | G | Restaurant | A1 |
| | | | | |
| Banquettes | | | | |
| B.G.01 | Banquette Detail | G | Restaurant | |
| | | | | |
| Tables and Chairs | | | | |
| TC.G.01 | Table Top Drawings -Square & Round | G | Restaurant | A1 |

# PAPER SIZES

Numerous paper sizes are used for the presentation of a working set of drawings. Within the United States, the standard layout is the **Architectural Classification**. Other formats consist of the **Engineering Format ANSI** (American national standards Institute) and in Europe and some other places, the A-series ISO 216 (international organization for Standardization).

| ANSI | Inches (") | Millimeters (mm) |
|---|---|---|
| A | 8.5 X 11 | 216 X 279 |
| B | 11 X 17 | 279 X 432 |
| C | 17 X 22 | 32 X 559 |
| D | 22 X 34 | 559 X 864 |
| E | 34 X 44 | 864 X 1,118 |

| Architectural | Inches (") | Millimeters (mm) |
|---|---|---|
| ARCH-A | 9 X 12 | 229 X 305 |
| ARCH-B | 12 X 18 | 305 X 457 |
| ARCH-C | 18 X 24 | 457 X 610 |
| ARCH-D | 24 X 36 | 610 X 914 |
| ARCH-E | 36 X 48 | 914 X 1,219 |

| ISO 216 | Inches (") | Millimeters (mm) |
|---|---|---|
| A0 | 33.125 X 46.75 | 841 X 1,189 |
| A1 | 23.375 X 33.125 | 594 X 841 |
| A2 | 16.5 X 23.375 | 420 X 594 |
| A3 | 11.75 X 16.5 | 297 X 420 |
| A4 | 8.25 X 11.375 | 210 X 297 |

### Relative Paper Sizes

The drawing below illustrates all of the paper sizes overlaid. The various ratios and sizes can be seen clearly.

### The ISO 216 Series

Each smaller paper size in the ISO series is derived by dividing in half the previous paper size parallel to its smaller side.

# WHAT ARE CONSTRUCTION DRAWINGS AND WHY WE NEED THEM

Construction drawings is the general term used for drawings that shape part of the production information, this is incorporated into tender documentation and then the contract documents for the construction work. This means they have legal significance and form part of the agreement among the client and the contractor. The main reason for construction drawings is to provide a graphic illustration of what is to be built. Construction drawings need to be concise and coordinated to avoid, wherever possible, uncertainty and confusion. Delays and misunderstandings can be minimized by adequately coordinating the drawings.

Specifications list the materials, sanitaryware, hardware and fabrics required to carry out the vision of the interior designer. Construction drawings provide the graphical description, indicating the arrangement of elements, details and dimensions. They will sometimes contain the information set out in specifications; however, this should be avoided if possible, by referring to specifications as opposed to repeating information. Where there is crossover, care needs to be taken to ensure correct co-ordination, so there is no confusion. If there is a difference between the two, the specifications will tend to take priority over the drawings.

A set of construction drawings tends to incorporate floor plans, elevations, sections and detail drawings, that collectively offer a complete illustration of the design. On various projects, a significant consultant may have their technical drawings specific to their trade, for example electrical, and plumbing.

Construction drawings can be prepared by hand; however, it's far more common for them to be prepared using computer-aided design (CAD) software.

# SETTING OUT A CONSTRUCTION PACKAGE

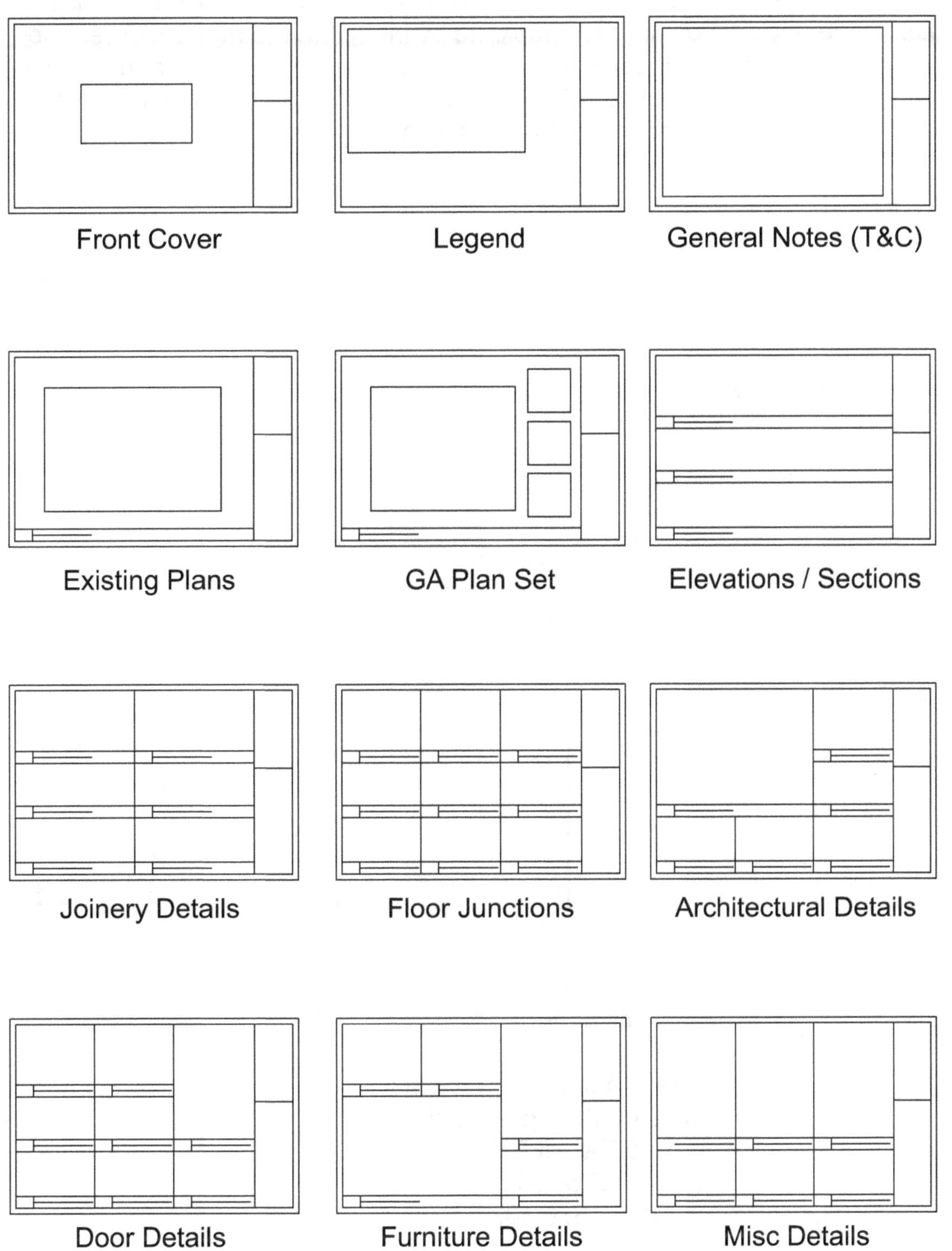

# FRONT COVER OF A DRAWING PACKAGE

The front cover is the first of the physical part of a construction package. It has one purpose: to identify the construction package by intriguing the right readers. The essential elements of a front cover include title, clients name, clients address, issue date and type of drawing package. Optional features include the subtitle (if there is one) and photos, background images or graphics.

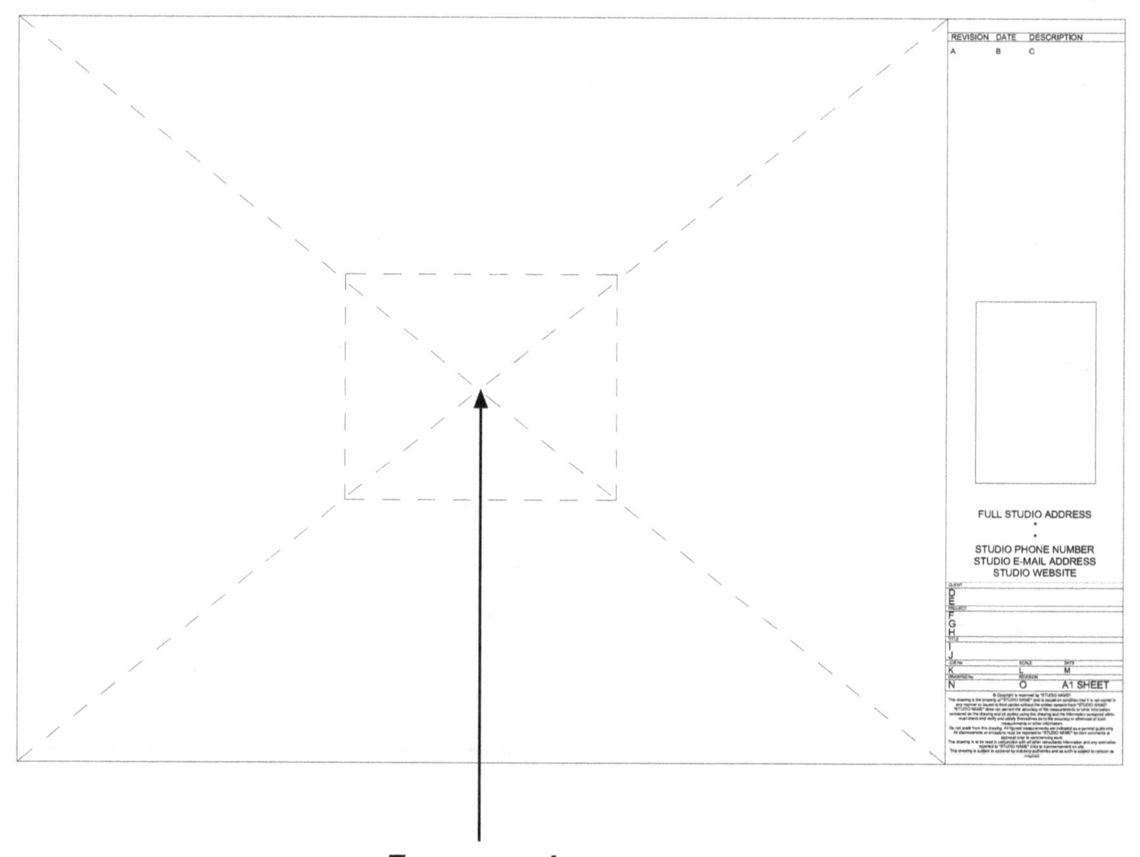


*For example:*

Hirthe, Bartoletti and Ebert
Unit 4, 68  Annfield Rd
BEACHLEY
NP6 4JT
079 4579 1091

# LEGENDS

The References, legend, Codes and Notations page is always placed on the second page of a drawing package. The purpose of the legend is to define all symbols, codes and hatches placed within a specific plan. A symbol may have more than one purpose. It has to be noted that all symbols used are typically not from a single standard. The crucial thing is that the interior designer, client and contractor understands the significance of the symbols on the drawing. This legend will give them that understanding.

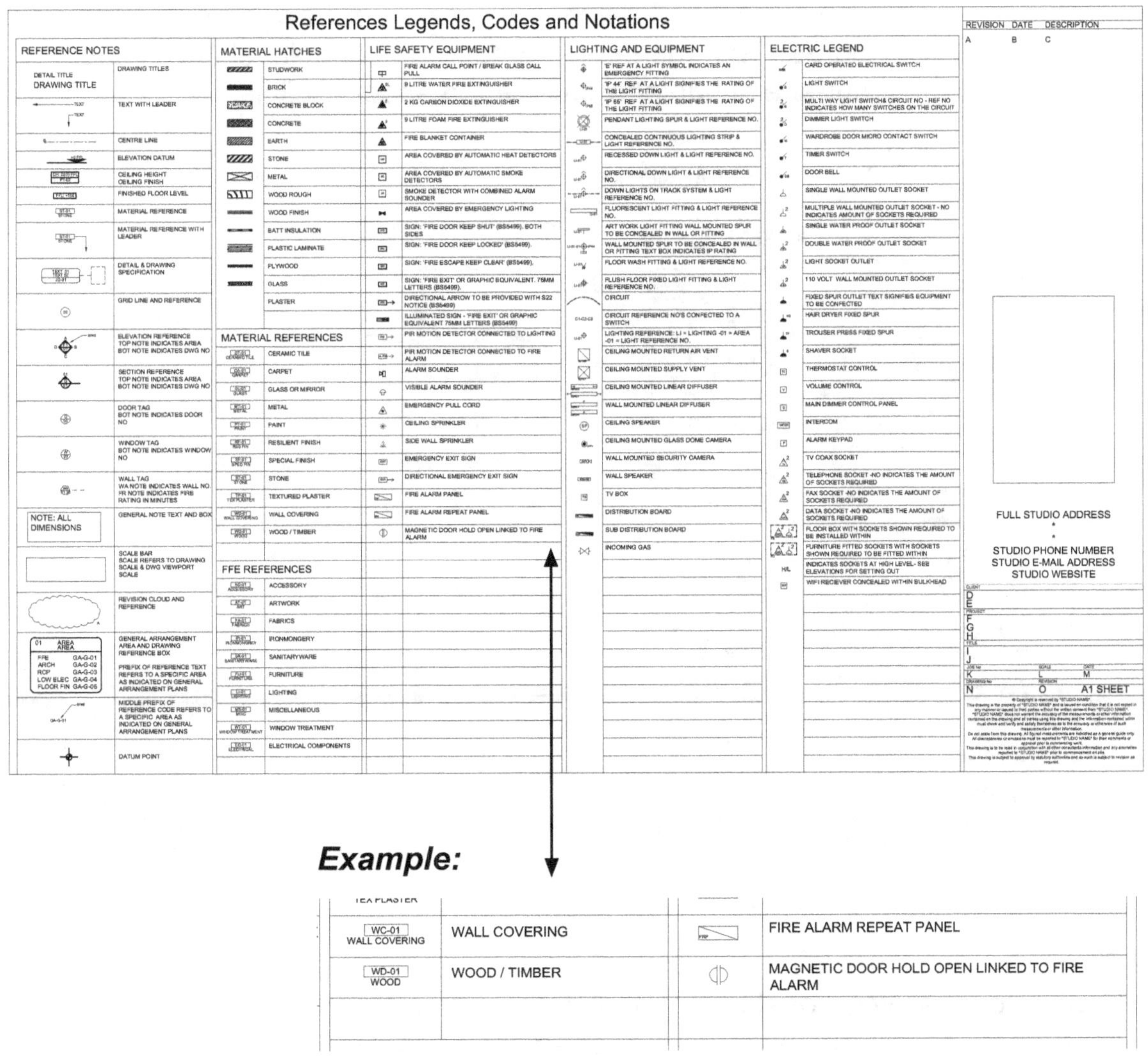

**Example:**

| | | | |
|---|---|---|---|
| WC-01 WALL COVERING | WALL COVERING | | FIRE ALARM REPEAT PANEL |
| WD-01 WOOD | WOOD / TIMBER | | MAGNETIC DOOR HOLD OPEN LINKED TO FIRE ALARM |

# GENERAL NOTES

General Notes, or GN's as they are usually referred to, include so much detail they are on the verge of becoming a form of specification. It is typically a shorter version of your Terms and Conditions, with the addition of includes notes that are needed within every package—covering the interior designer, client, contractor and specialist-contractors.

**Example:**
In areas where an unevenness in surfaces occurs, contractor shall patch and repair or renew the surface as agreed with the I.D to produce a plumb, level and smooth surface suitable to receive the specified finish.

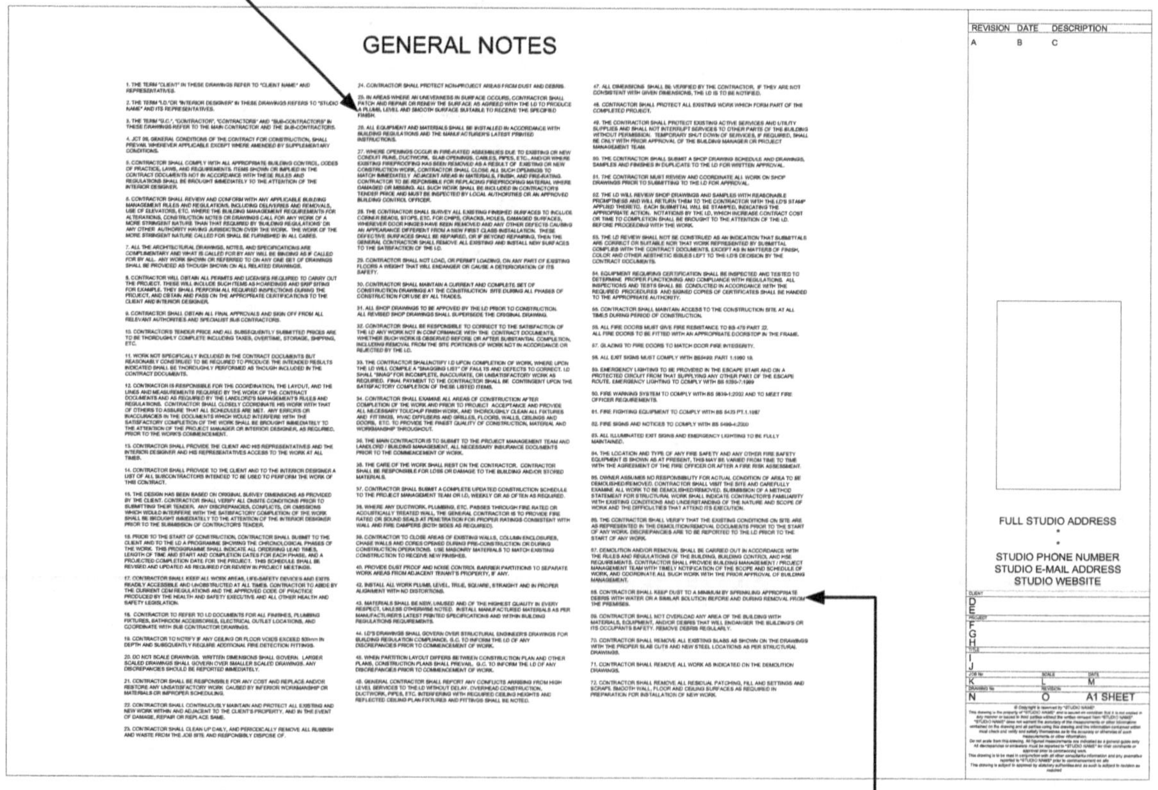

**Example:**
Contractor shall keep dust to a minimum by sprinkling appropriate debris with water or similar solution before and during removal from the premises.

# THE TITLE BLOCK OF EVERY DRAWING

When starting a formal set of drawings for client approval, planning or construction purposes, there's one recurring element this is required on every drawing sheet, this is a 'Title Block'. The information that identifies an overall understanding of the project and information to do with only the particular drawing.

*A* - Revision Number (A,B,C,D..).
*B* - Date the revised drawing was issued.
*C* - Short description of the revision.
*D* - Client/s name.
*E* - Client/s official office address.
*F* - Project name.
*G* - Project's full site address 1.
*H* - Project's full site address 2.
*I* - Title of drawing 1.
*J* - Title of drawing 2.
*K* - In-house studio job-number*.
*L* - Scale of the drawing within the sheet.
*M* - Date of first issue (will not change after revisions)
*N* - Drawing number (GA.G.00 for example)
*O* - Current revision of drawing, to correspond with sections A, B and C.

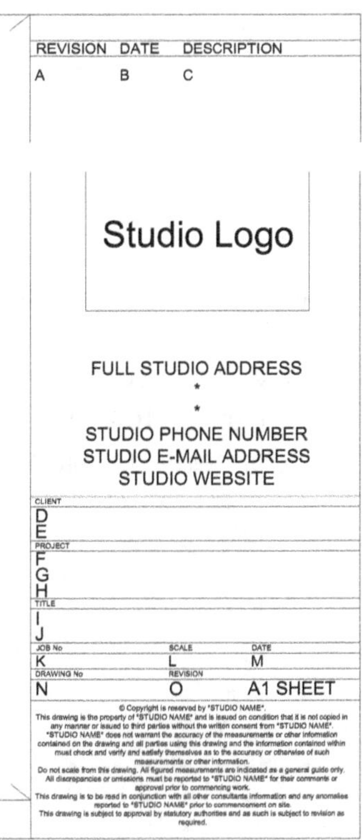


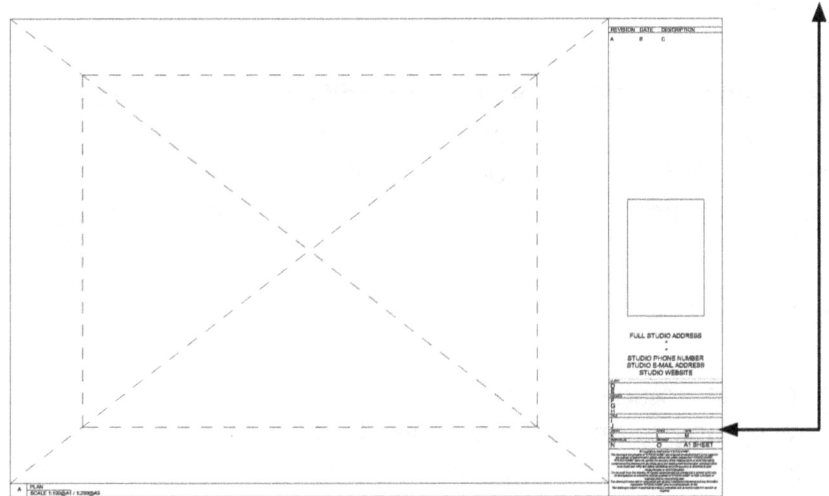

# HOW TO FOLD AN A1 DRAWING SHEET

The purpose of folding large interior or architectural drawings is to allow the lower portion of the title block to be seen while not having to open the whole sheet. Allowing a stack of drawings to be filed and then easily identified with the aid of the sheet number and drawing title.

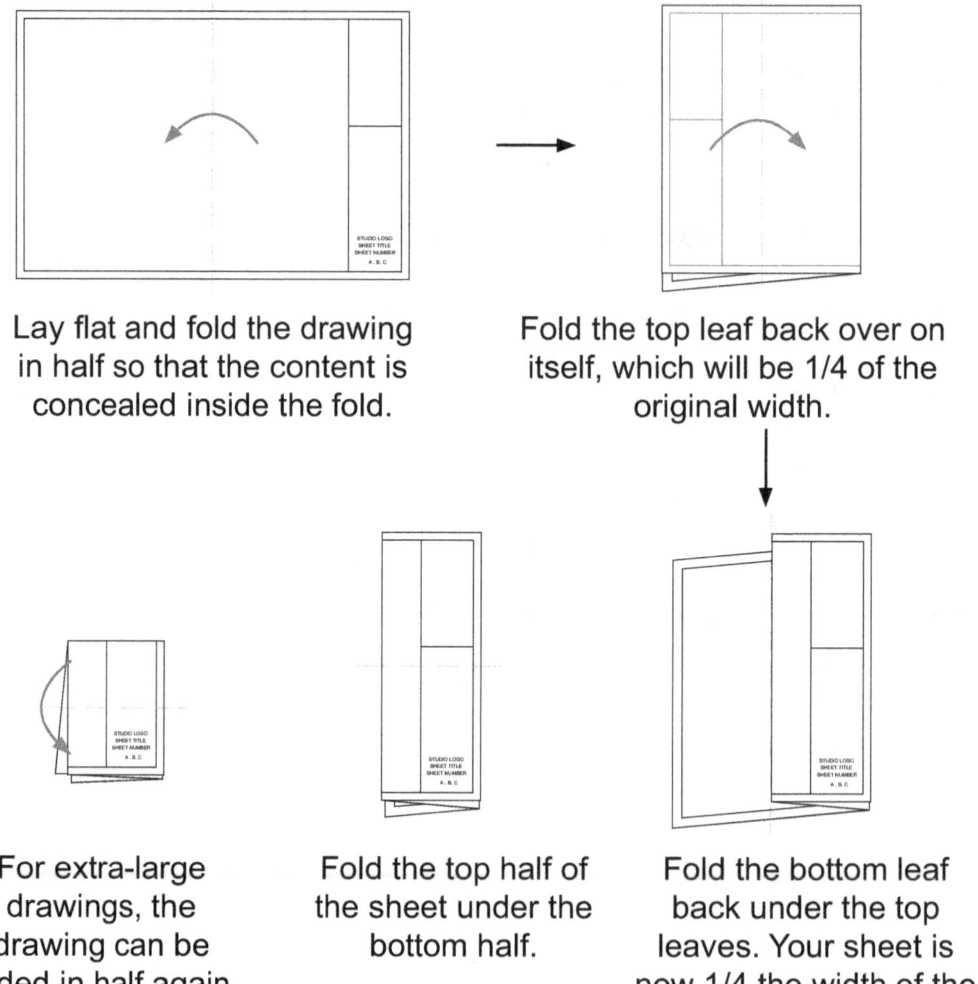

Lay flat and fold the drawing in half so that the content is concealed inside the fold.

Fold the top leaf back over on itself, which will be 1/4 of the original width.

For extra-large drawings, the drawing can be folded in half again.

Fold the top half of the sheet under the bottom half.

Fold the bottom leaf back under the top leaves. Your sheet is now 1/4 the width of the full sheet.

***Why fold in this way?***

-The fold produces an A4 sheet size.
-The folded drawing opens and closes easier that other types of folding.
-The drawing title is on the front. Thus you do not have to open the entire sheet to see what the drawing is.

# TYPES OF DRAWINGS IN INTERIOR DESIGN

Drawings are the primary communicative tool in an interior designer's pocket. A few drawing types will overlap with the ones in other disciplines, such as an architect or electrical engineer's, while others are specific to interior design. The subsequent pages show the standard drawings with which an interior designer should be familiar.

## *General Arrangement Plan*

This floor plan establishes the limits from demise lines to exterior walls that will frame the project—showing the complete layout for the project including all furniture, mill-work, partitions, sanitaryware, kitchen layouts, any external works and circulation routes. The plan is generally clean to have general discussions and mark any revisions while with the client.

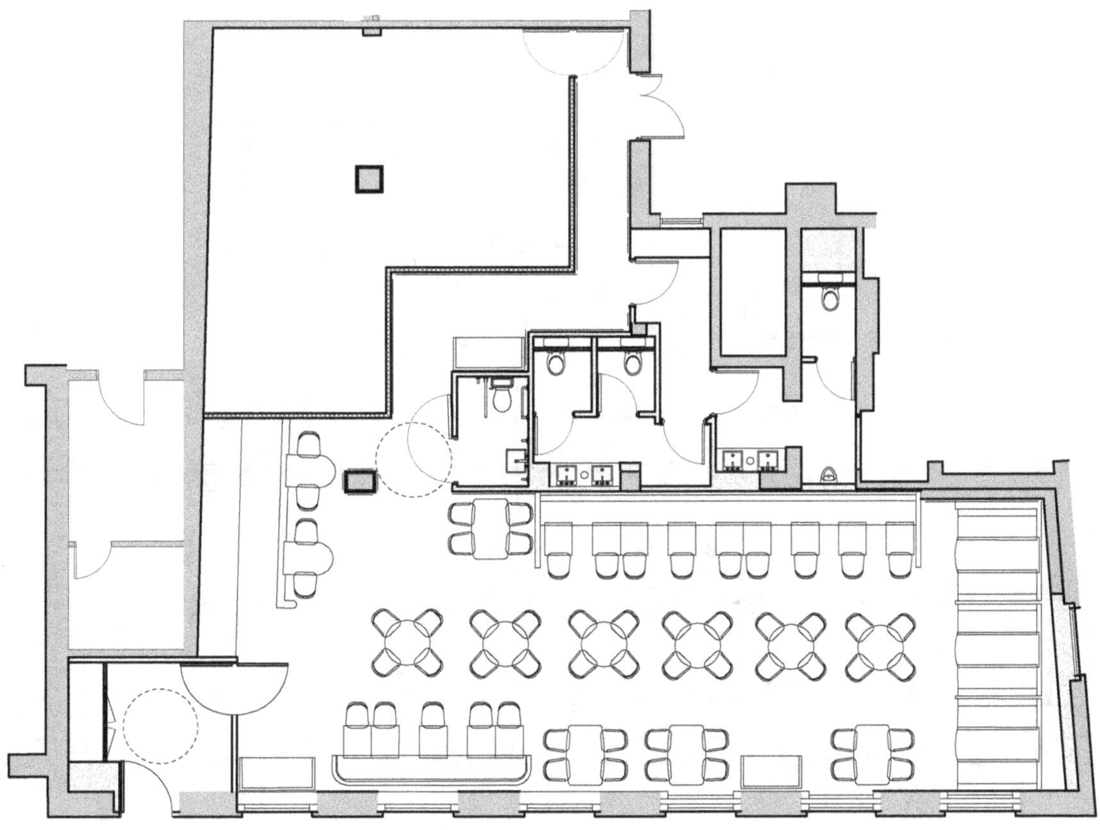

## Furniture Plan

The same plan set as the 'General Arrangement Plan' but this is where we indicate every piece of furniture, mill-work and indicate their corresponding drawing if needed. Codes, Furniture Names, Quantity and Notes are also added in a Legend for easy reading. Dimensions are added to any critical areas, for example, any pinch points and design crucial dimensions.

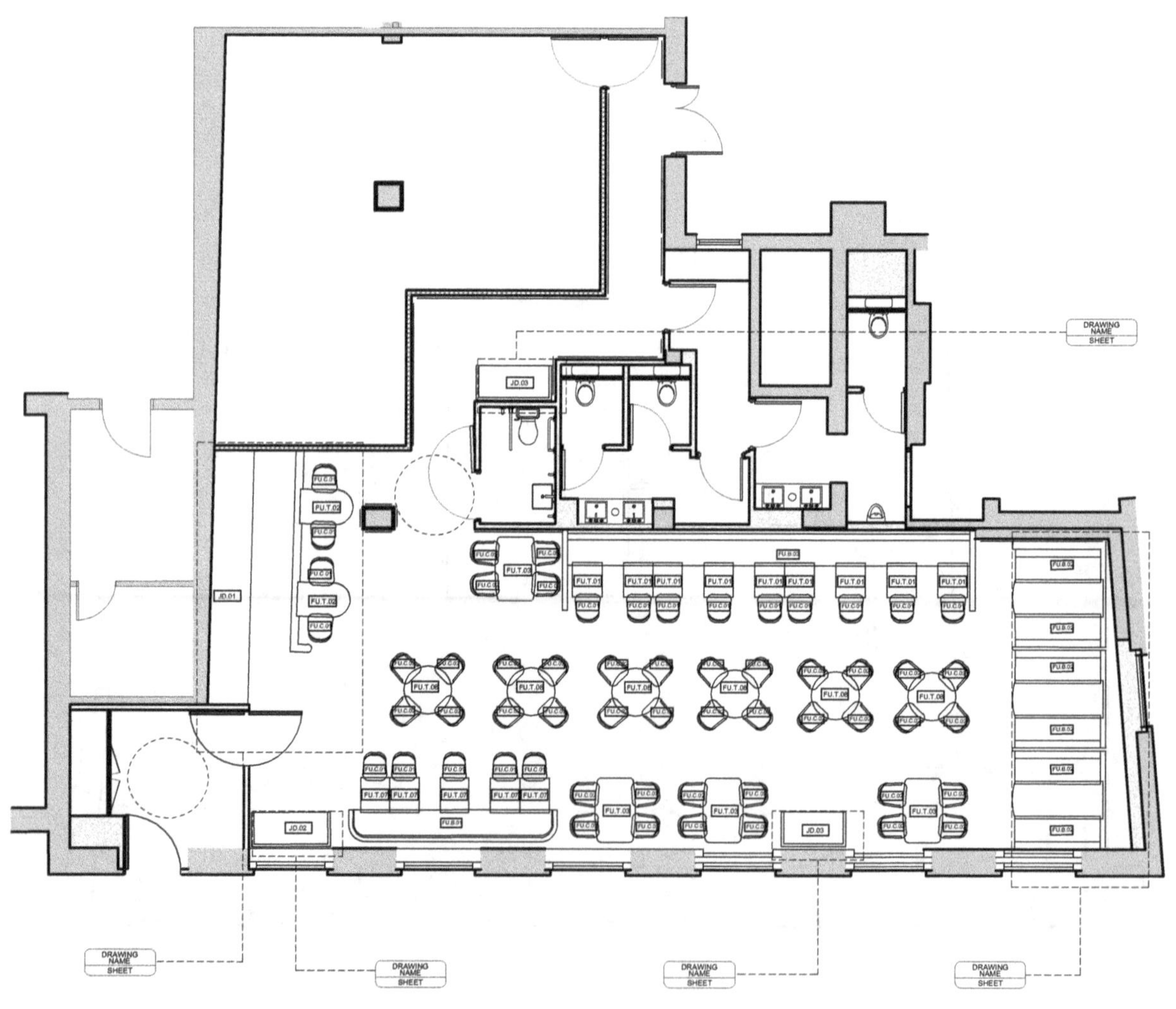

## Demolition Plan

The Demolition Plan shows the existing state of the building, a vital drawing for any contractor. It is covered with notes for what will need to be removed (and protected/ preserved) to make way for new construction. These sections are usually shown in a <u>red dashed line</u>. All new partitions are also shown with dimensions for setting out on-site, but are shown in their standard line weights.

### A Note about Dimensioning

When dimensioning, stand in the place of a contractor, what dimensions would you need to construct the partitions? This way of working creates a much easier to read the plan.

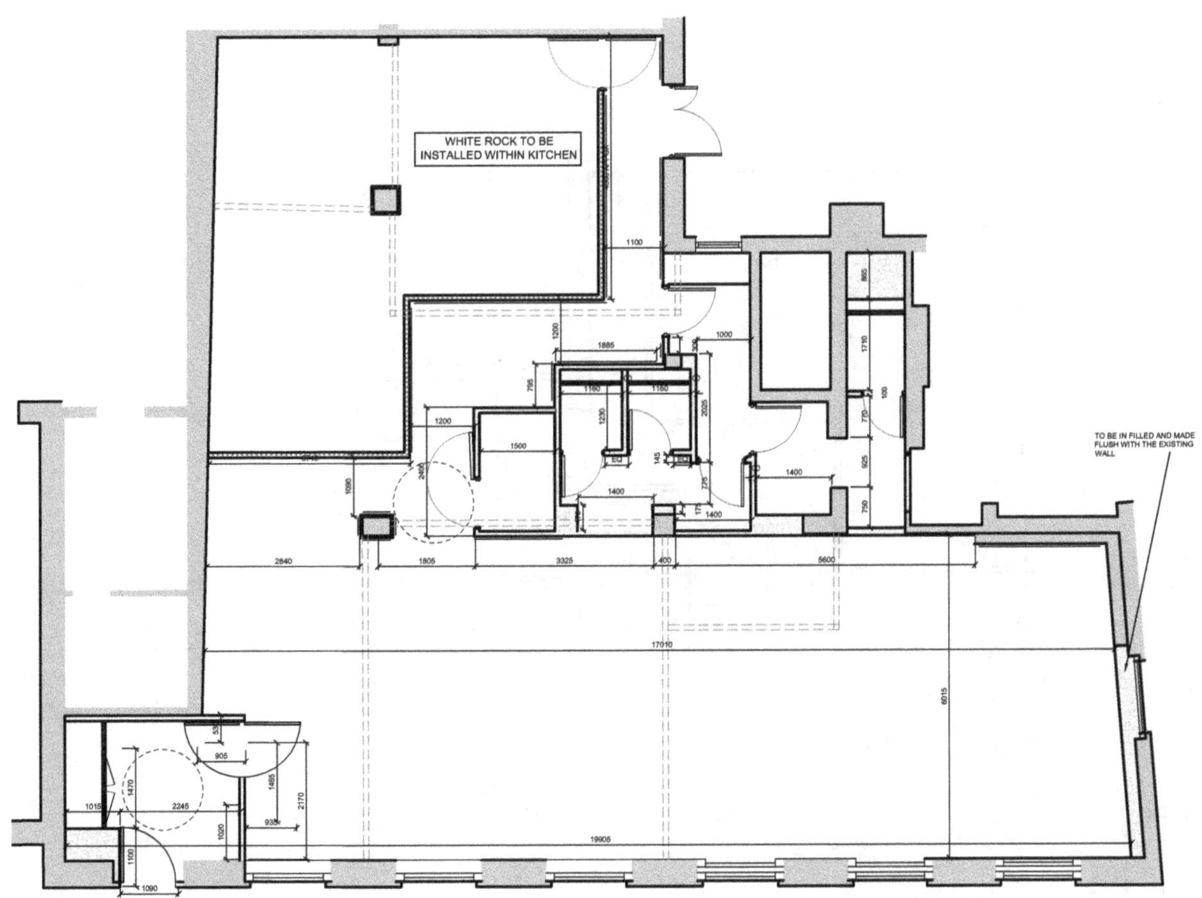

# Reflected Ceiling Plans

A reflected ceiling plan (RCP) depicts the upper surface of a space as considered through a mirror. All electrical and lighting fixtures, beams, and other ceiling information, including ceiling heights and materials are shown on RCPs. Standard symbols and tags are used to describe fixture types and locations are marked to a legend on the drawing.

*A legend is added to the page indicating which lights will be linked together, forming a lighting circuit. Helping the contractor with installing dimming zooms and lighting levels. The lighting code "HL-02" or a curved line connecting the lighting can be used to indicate this.*

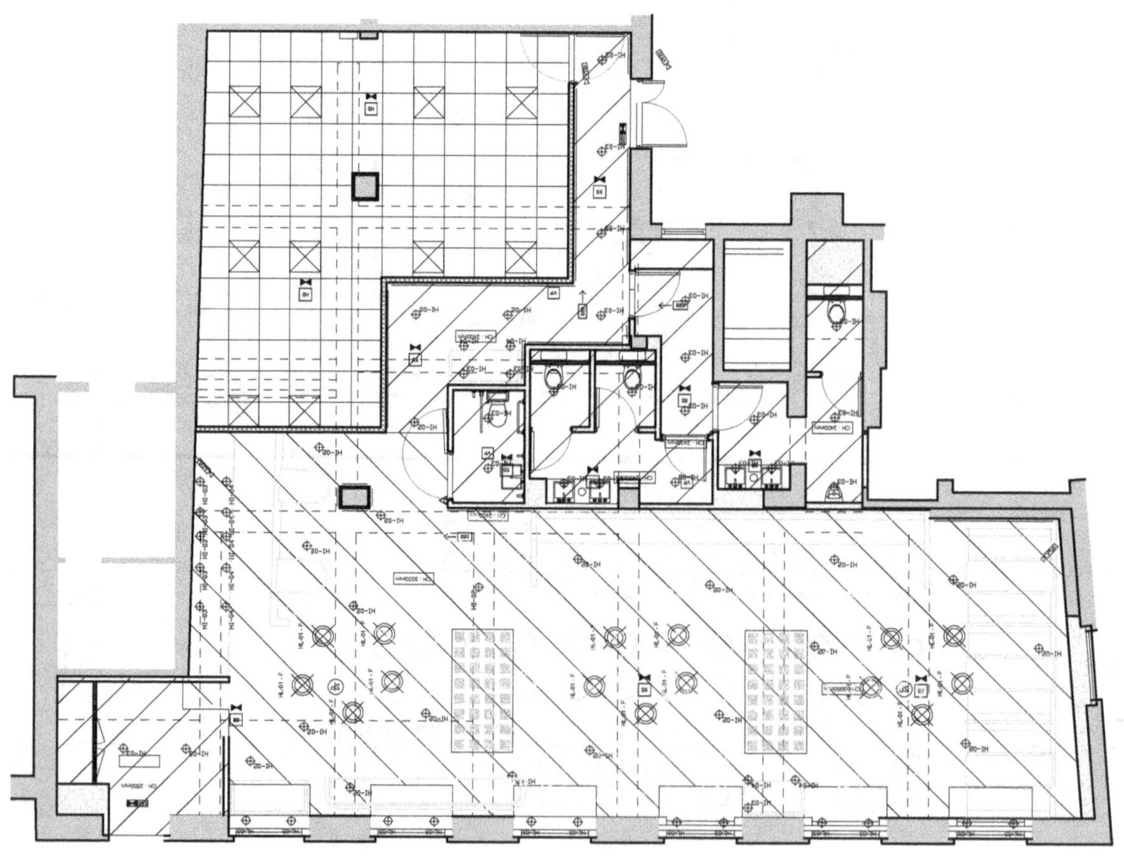

## Low Level Electrical Plan

The low-level electrical plan indicates all furnishings and mill-work in a light grey line weight. All wall sconces, electrical sockets, mill-work power and data requirements and emergency systems are all shown on the plan and dimensioned. Standard symbols are used to explain fixture types and location and are marked to a legend on the drawing.

High Level is indicated with (HL), and this is everything above counter height, Low Level is indicated with (LL), and this is everything below counter height.

*A legend is added to the page indicating which lights will be linked together, forming a lighting circuit. Helping the contractor with installing dimming zooms and lighting levels. The lighting code "HL-02" or a curved line connecting the lighting needs to be used to indicate this.*

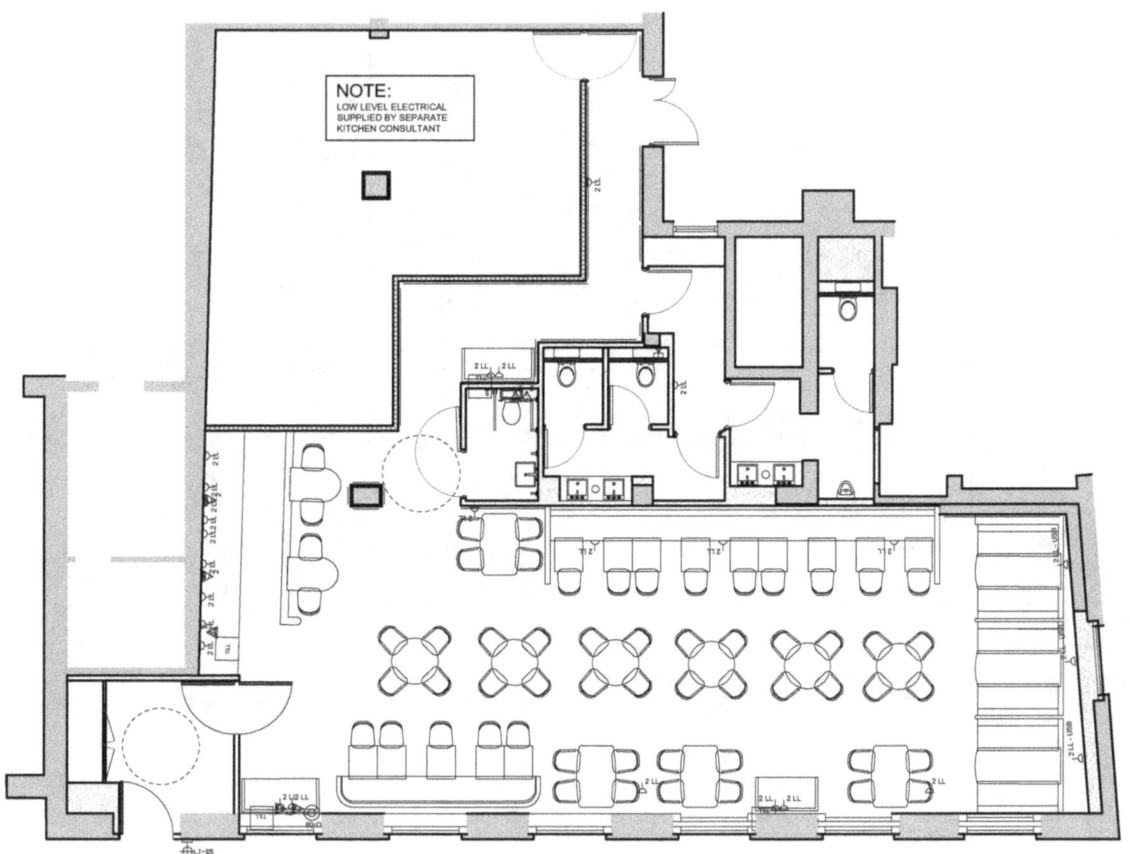

## *Floor Finish Plans*

Floor finishes plan describes the various finishes used in a project. The finishes are dimensioned as necessary. Standard symbols and hatches that identify finish types are linked to a legend that accompanies each plan.

Using a hatch that closely resembles the selected flooring choice; this will both help in showing if the scale will work within a space and identify each flooring zone.

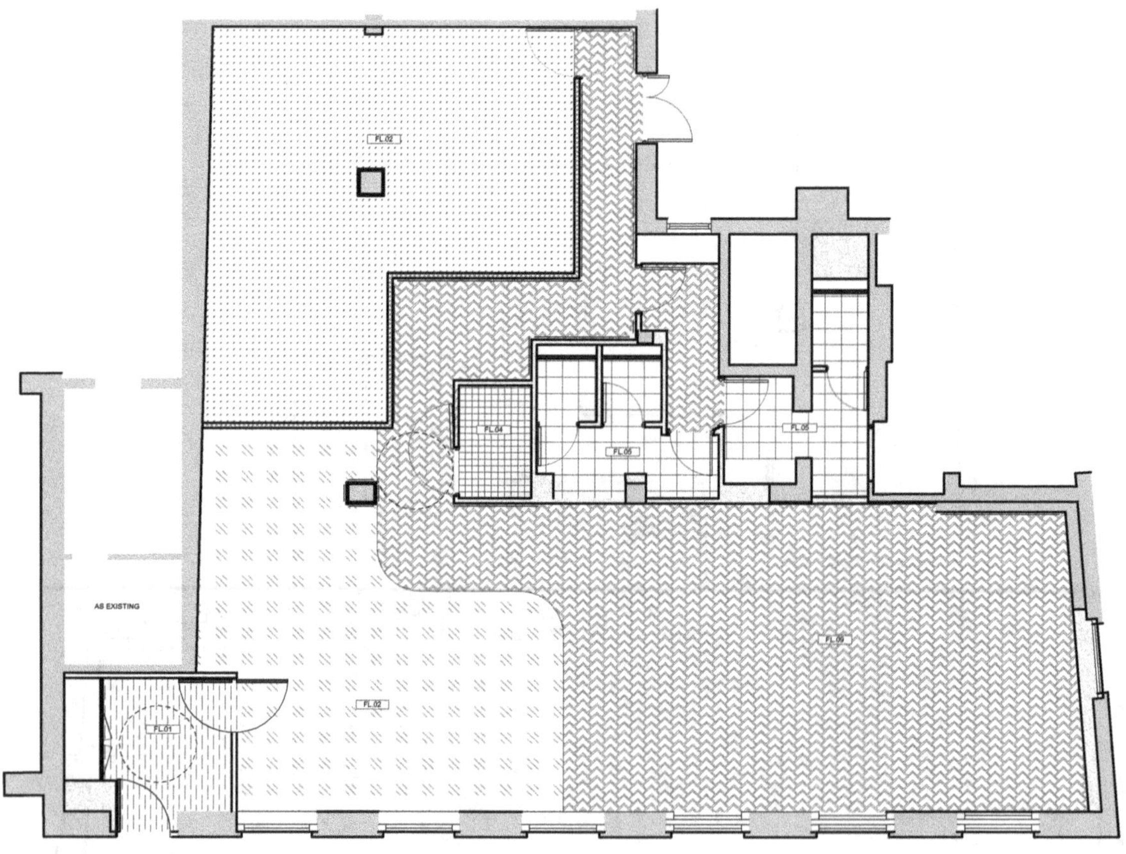

# INTERIOR ELEVATIONS

Elevations are generally drawn at a larger scale than the plans of the project. Allows for the inclusion of extra elements, which include precise information about the dimensional and material characteristics of objects in the design. Elements on elevational drawings are cross-referenced to section and plan details that further develop the design. Here, transoms, cabinets, door and glazing details, and custom furniture are highlighted with the aid of a call-out.

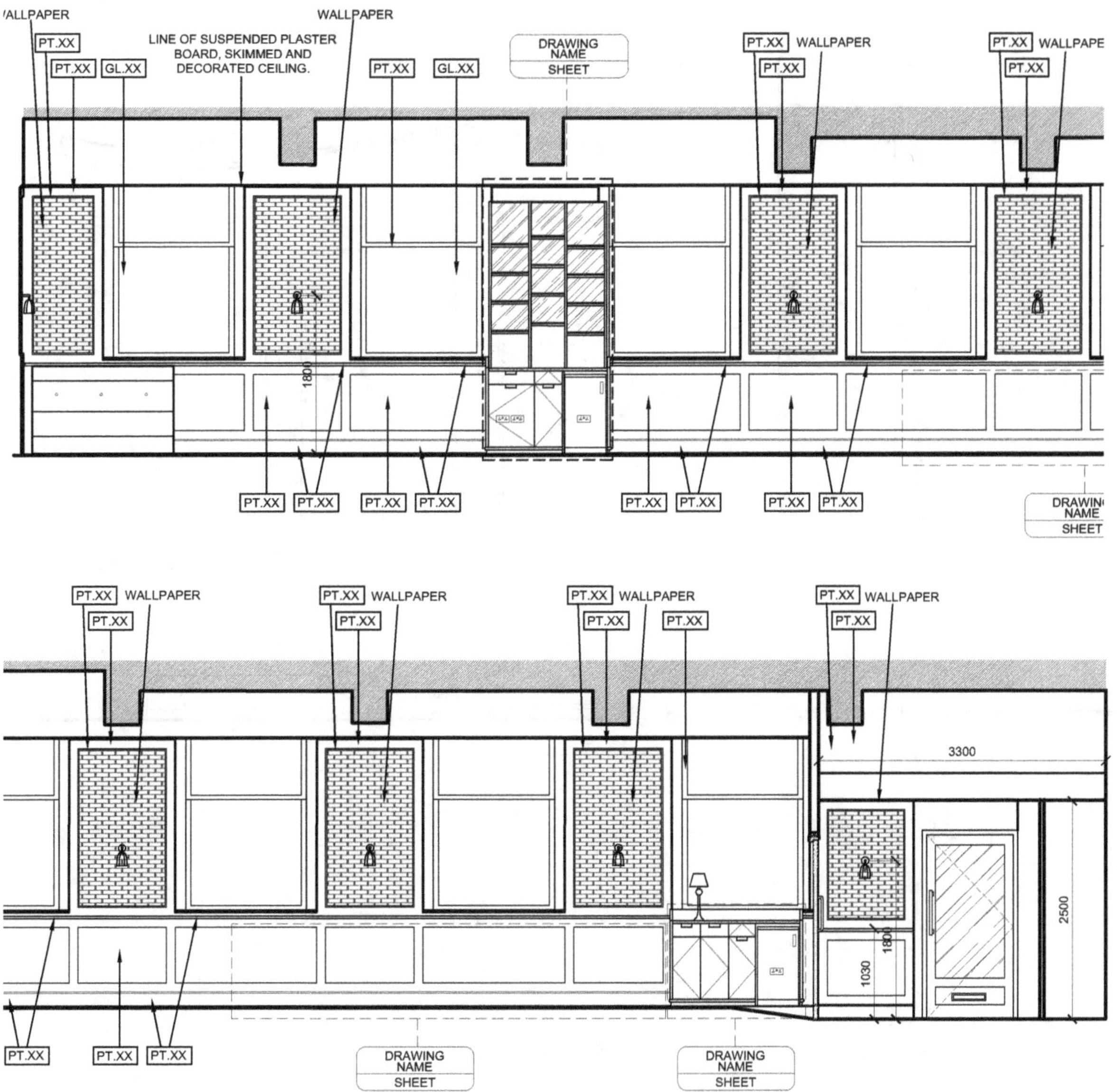

# DETAILS

Details indicate how the design is to be fabricated and range from wall sections to mechanical coordination details to mill-work construction. They are produced at a larger scale than all other drawings in the package. Scales for details can be as small as (1:10) through to full scale (1:1). Occasionally, details are drawn at larger than full scale to transmit the intent of the designer to the fabricator or contractor. This would be a scale of (2:1) two times larger or (5:1) five times larger. In detail drawings, materials are rendered symbolically, and annotations specify the material and fabrication methods to be used.

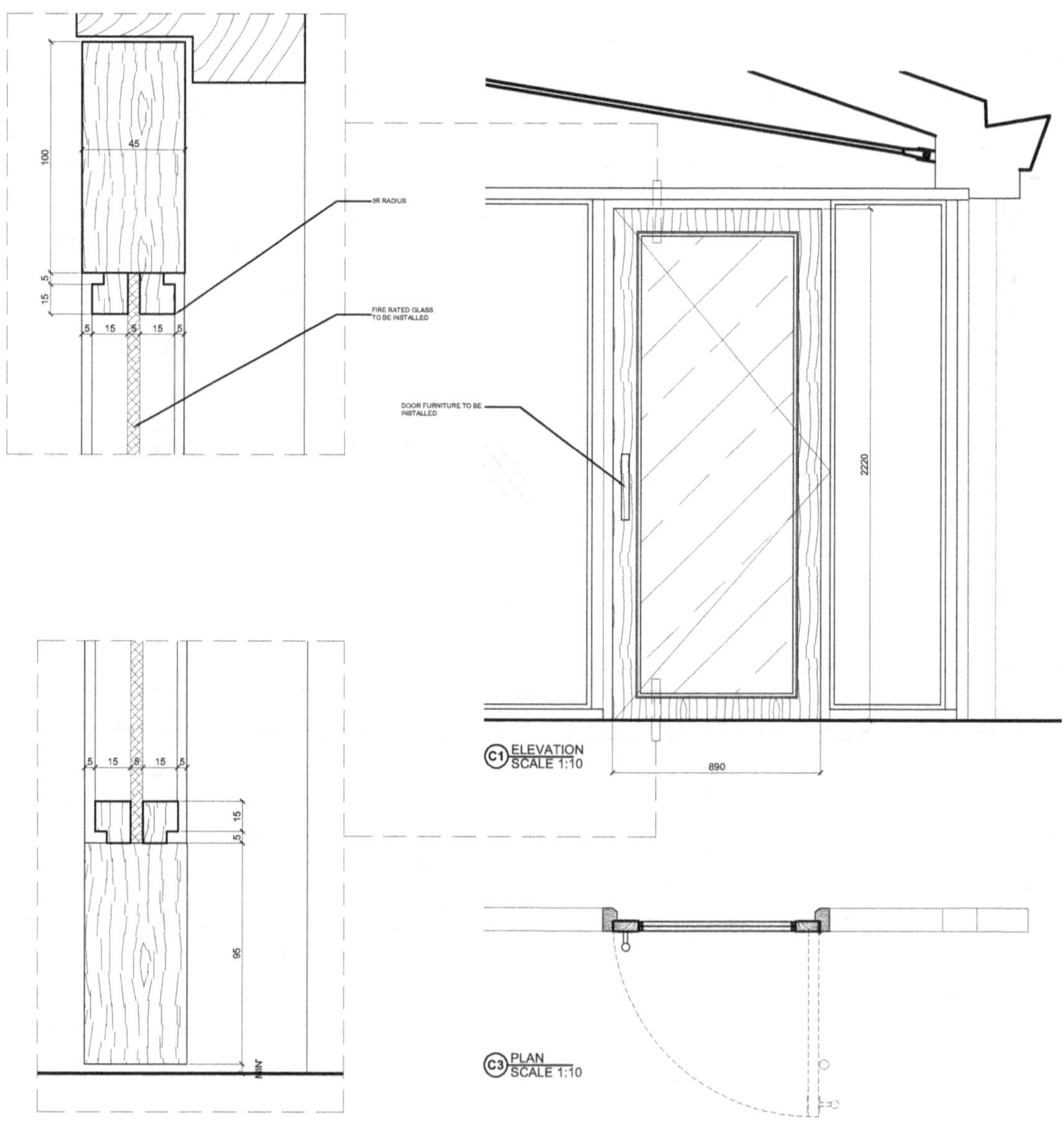

# LAYERING AND STANDARDS

The sharing of information across users, both within an interior design studio and among consultants, requires a close agreement on how layers are named and organized. Several organizations have developed strategies for systems that facilitate information interchange. The National CAD Standard and the AIA Layer Guidelines are two prominent ones, though several other layering systems exist. A strategy for layer use and formatting is usually agreed upon during the contract negotiation phase of a project.

The National CAD Standard also covers the annotation of drawing sets, model files, and sheet files. The drawing below demonstrates the system as deployed by the NCS:

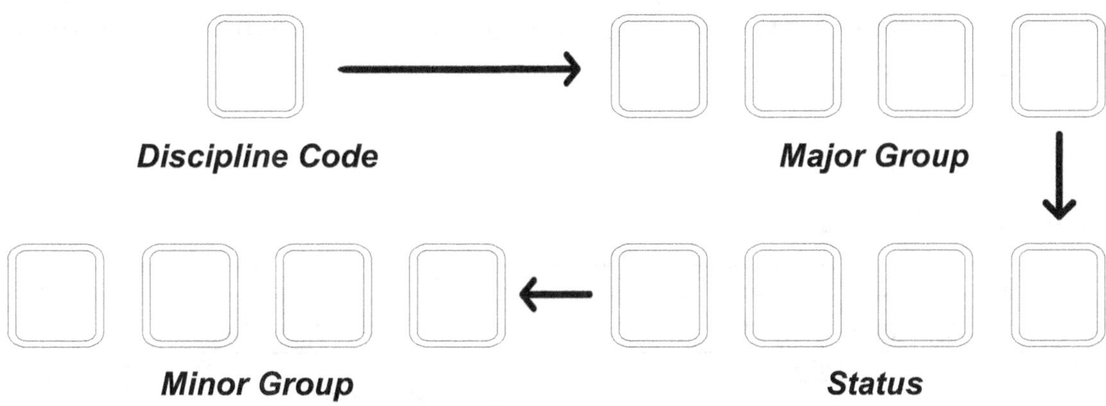


Any combination of a discipline code and a major group constitutes a suitable layer naming convention. As an example, a standard layer breakdown will be as follows:

WALL-DEMO to suggest a layer for interior walls that are to be demolished WALL-INTR to identify a layer for new interior walls

Normal layer formats within the interior design profession include, however, are not restricted to:
A-AREA, A-CEILING, A-DEFPOINTS, A-DEMOLITION, A-DIMS, A-DOORS, A-DRAINAGE, A-ELECTRICAL, A- FLOORING, A-FURNITURE, A-JOINERY, A-LANDSCAPE, A-TEXT, A-WALLS, A-WINDOWS

(Notice: The 'A' designation is usually used for initials of the design studio, however as there is a lot of overlap amongst disciplines, it is best to keep the standard consistent.

# TRANSLATION AND LIMITATIONS

Most three-dimensional modelling applications write files in a format native to their application; but, several file export types are available for use with other platforms and programs. As with two-dimensional applications, the most common are DXF' and DWG', which, being proprietary to Autodesk, are at risk of change with every new launch. Other formats include XML, OBJ, and 3DS. BIM models are increasingly being shared through the open format industry.

### *A Note about Tablet-based Applications*
With the rise of portable devices, many drawing and preliminary 3D modelling applications have become available to the designer. These applications have many of the benefits of their desktop counterparts, including layering, vector and raster drawing, and export options. The addition of a stylus has made both beginning the design process, hand sketching, markup, and communication viable away from the constraints of a desktop machine.

## *3-D Modelling Software*

| Program | | Solid | Surfaces | Amination | Operating System | Paid | Free |
|---|---|---|---|---|---|---|---|
| AutoCAD | (CAD) | O | O | | Windows, MacOS | ££££ | |
| 3D Studio Max | (3DS) | O | O | O | Windows | ££££ | |
| Bender 3D | (B3D) | | O | O | Windows, MacOS | | O |
| Cinema 4D | (C4D) | O | O | O | Windows, MacOS | ££££ | |
| Rhinocereos | (Rhino) | | O | | Windows, MacOS | ££ | |
| Sketch-Up | (SUP) | O | O | O | Windows, MacOS | ££ | O |

## *Building Information Software*

| Program | | Solid | Surfaces | Amination | Operating System | Paid | Free |
|---|---|---|---|---|---|---|---|
| Revit | (REV) | O | O | O | Windows | ££££ | |
| ArchiCAD | (AICAD) | O | O | O | Windows, MacOS | ££££ | |

## *Online (Via Browser)*

| Program | | Solid | Surfaces | Amination | Operating System | Paid | Free |
|---|---|---|---|---|---|---|---|
| OnShape | (ONS) | O | | | Browser (Internet) | | O |
| My.Sketch | (MYS) | O | O | O | Browser (Internet) | | O |
| TrinkerCAD | (TRCAD) | O | | | Browser (Internet) | | O |

## CHAPTER FOUR

# PRESENTATION AND COMMUNICATION

Interior drawings perform more than one task for the interior designer. They help communicate their ideas to the client at the start of any project, they present the vision and content of the designer at strategic points in the process, and they are also vital to the construction phase in the form of a drawing package. Their effectiveness, however, depends on how they are presented. Designers have a selection of presentation methods and styles available to them, all of which have unique features within the design process. Anything an interior designer communicates to the public must be taken into consideration as a reflection of the design studio. Some referred to as branding; it is a name, term, sign, symbol or design. A combination of them intend to identify the products and services of a design, a combination of these intend to identify the goods and services of a design studio and to differentiate them from their competition. Letterheads, Business Cards, Proposals, Brochures, Design Boards and Projected Images all serve to speak the designers vision. It is crucial to develop clean and graphically attractive program, regardless of the scale of the project or how the work is being presented.

## DEVELOPING A PRESENTATION

A key skill for an interior designer is the ability to develop an appealing and successful presentation that translates the ideas and notions that led to specific design decisions. Create a narrative with a story outlining and storyboarding the presentation, determining the appropriate medium for the content are a few of the interior designer's tasks.

The designer must also know how drawings used as graphic elements function within different types of presentations, and how the basics of graphic design can influence the designers presentation. Keep an updated library of image references that not only offer inspiration but also provide strong examples of layout and narrative development, and graphic design magazines are a perfect starting point. Keep in mind the relatively recent appearance of high-quality colour prints even from fairly inexpensive inkjet printers has expanded the resources available for presenting ideas in printed form. It is vital that the interior designer takes a look at how the format of a print can affect the translation of design and how to draw on graphic skills to support this communication.

# DESIGN BOARDS

Design boards set a regular and ordered structure in which the intent of the concept is represented. For boards to be successful, principle storyboarding must be applied to the information being presented; this involves the balance of the elements on the board itself and the flow in which the narrative unfolds. Design boards allow the client to spend a great deal of time examining the work, and for that reason, elements need to be paced to allow for further discovery the longer they are examined. Many issues need to be considered while designing the presentation boards.

### *Number of Boards:*

When determining the number of boards needed in a presentation, numerous questions must be asked: What is the size and scale of the project? How many drawings will be required to explain the project? Are there going to be perspectives, if so how many? Will samples be attached directly to the board or scanned and added to a board?

### *Spacing, Scale, and Speed:*

When producing the layout for a presentation, it is essential to consider how the boards will be viewed. Some clients will quickly scan through the boards, and others will stop to look at the work in depth. By anticipating this, layout strategies regarding the spacing and scale of objects can begin to address the speed at which they are examined.

### *Narrative Development and Outlining:*

Creating a compelling narrative for the presentation means, telling a story of the design process as you would like it seen—a well written and ordered narrative structures what is needed to be in the presentation and when. Narratives provide a core value that can allocate emphasis and interest to specific aspects of the process. Maintaining an outline of the design, and developing it as the project evolves, will focus the narrative.

### *Orientation:*

Presentation boards arranged with their length vertically are said to be in portrait format and those with a width longer than height are referred to as landscape. Each has its benefits: Portrait - These type of boards have a visual resonance with the printed page and when displayed in sequence, allow for more information in less horizontal space. Landscape - These type of boards enable a more natural cropping for perspectives, and their width encourages a more informal sequencing.

***White Space:***
The white space that encompasses specific items on a sheet can be used to increase the relative importance of any drawing, sample, or text. Designers should always avoid overcomplicating the design of the presentation by overcrowding too much information and imagery too not enough boards.
***Remember*** - Adding another board is always an option.

***Storyboarding and Thumbnails:***
A useful technique for developing the presentation is to create multiple versions known as mock-ups. These mock-ups gather the information to be presented and then explore several sequencing strategies.

***Labeling and Annotation:***
Often being overlooked, but one of the essential factors in deciding how a layout is noticed is the choice of a font that will translate the designer's text. Clear, readable type, used at different type sizes, can add another layer to how a board is read; it also offers another graphic element for the design of the board. Establishing a good selection of fonts early in the process allows annotations to be placed with the graphics in specific ways. At the very least, decisions should be made concerning the following label types in a document: title font, label font, and caption font.

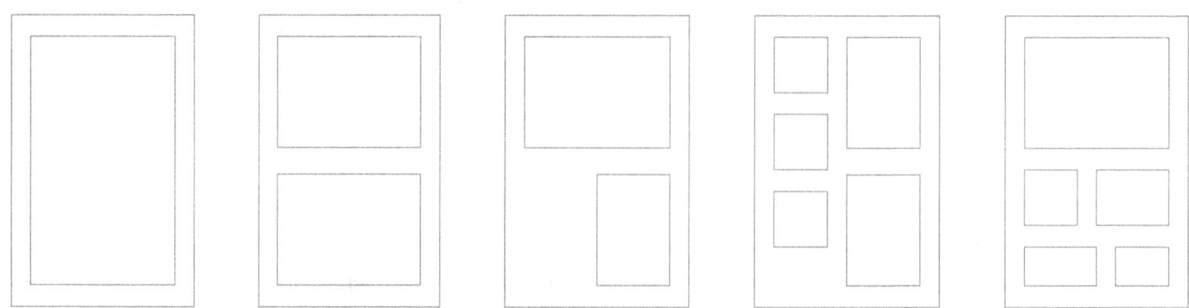

# GRID DEVELOPMENT

Establishing the structure and placement of items on a presentation board, the interior designer should develop a template that implements rules within the form of grids. Grids, when set up correctly, can make clear the appearance and number of the design objects. If unsure where to start, interior designers can draw from graphic design, from which the following examples come to style their grid systems.

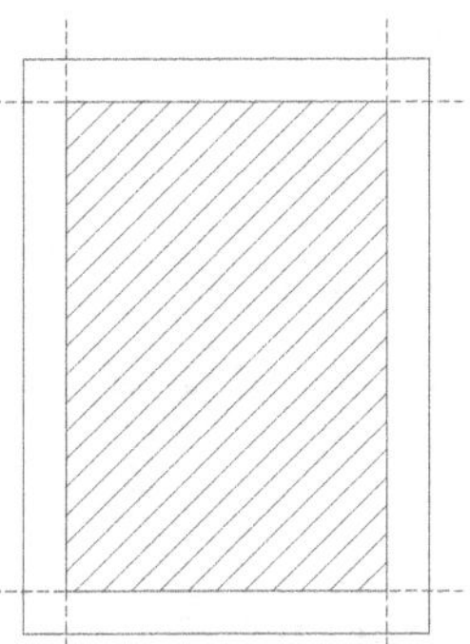

***Single Box:***
Singular content, such as a rendered plan or perspective.

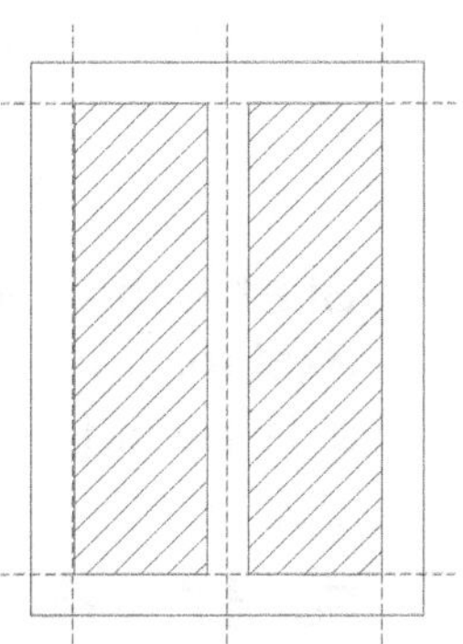

***Multi-Box:***
Allows for multiple images and text

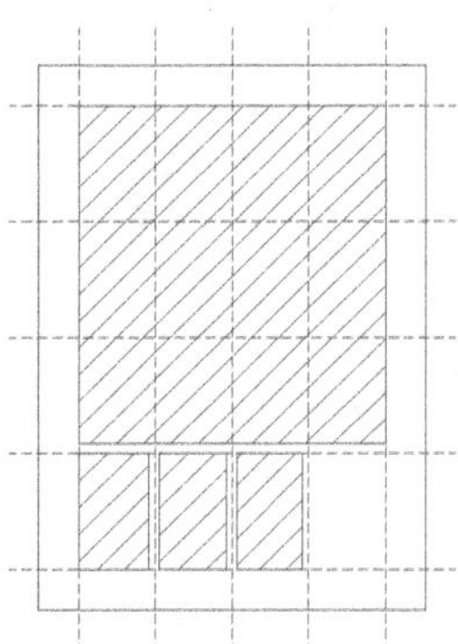

***Anchored:***
Content, including images, titles, anchors the page.

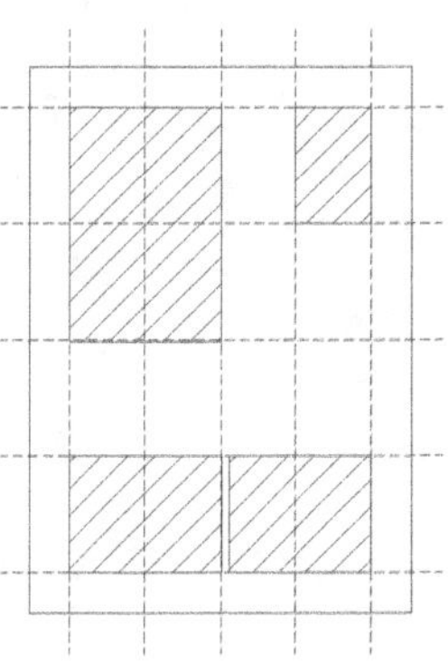

***Modular:***
Comprehensive grids that allow for variation in placement of elements.

## LAYOUT STRATEGIES (GRID)

The following examples illustrate how a modular grid system can be adapted into a larger set of design boards.

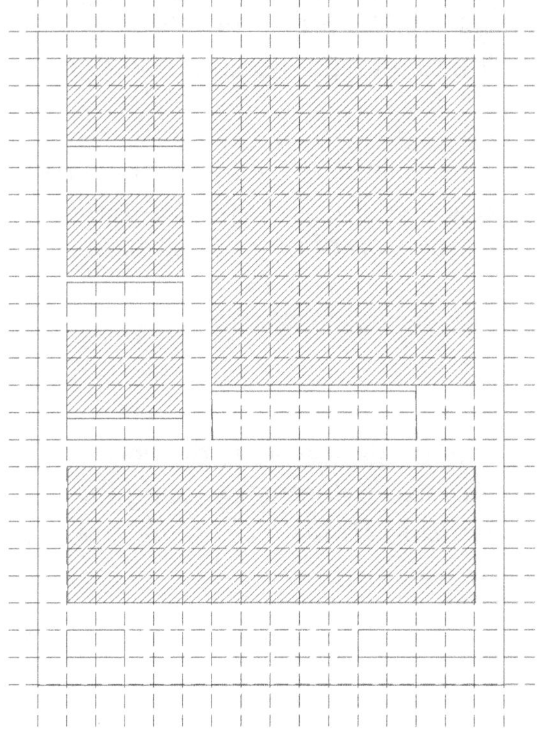

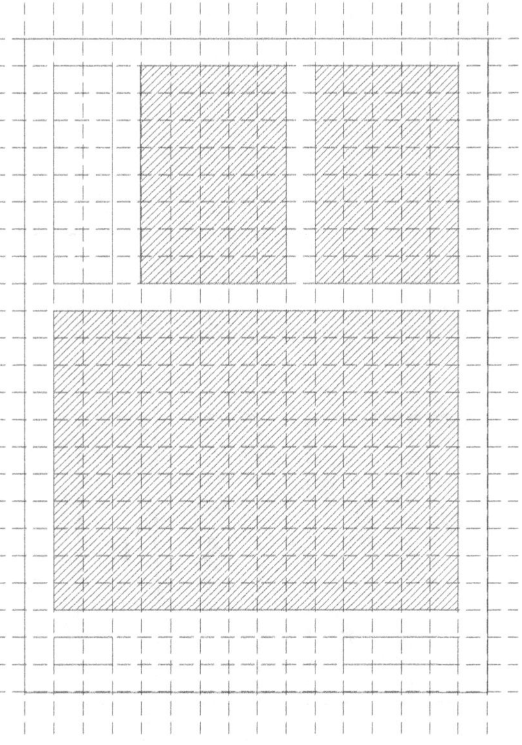

# LAYOUT STRATEGIES (TRIANGLE)

The perfect presentation is how designers describe this technique. This way of laying out a presentation existed long before a computer, the printing process or even a defined measuring unit. No points, inches or millimetres, it could be produced with nothing greater than a straight edge, a piece of paper and a pencil.

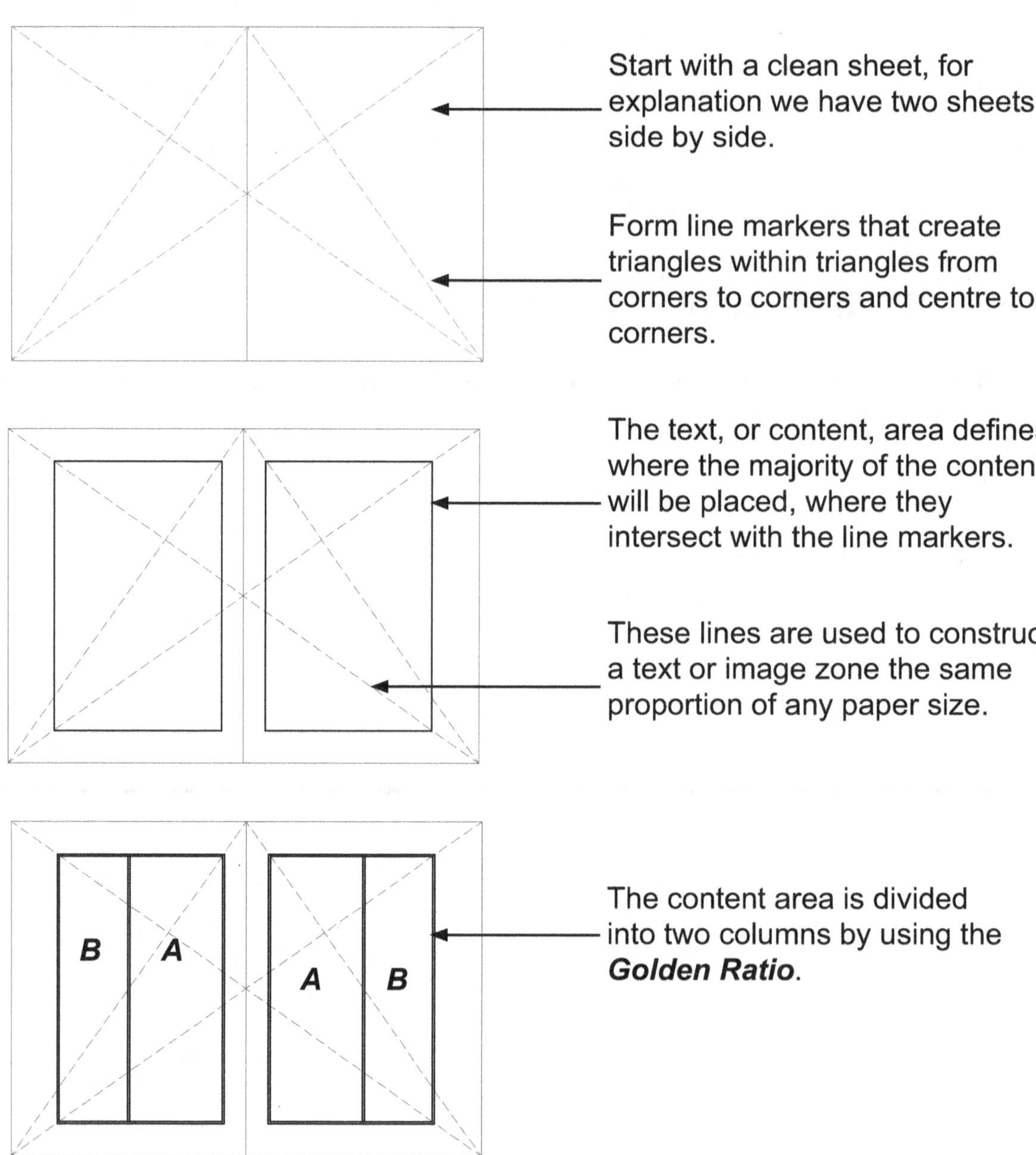

Start with a clean sheet, for explanation we have two sheets side by side.

Form line markers that create triangles within triangles from corners to corners and centre to corners.

The text, or content, area defines where the majority of the content will be placed, where they intersect with the line markers.

These lines are used to construct a text or image zone the same proportion of any paper size.

The content area is divided into two columns by using the *Golden Ratio*.

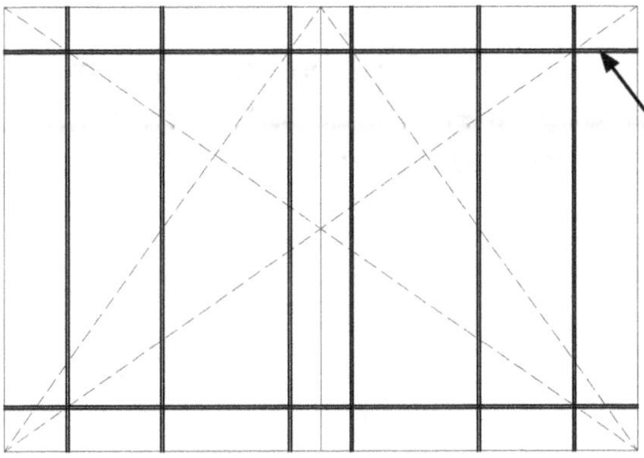

Extending the lines out to the edge of the sheet from the content area, this begins to give the designer more of a complete grid.

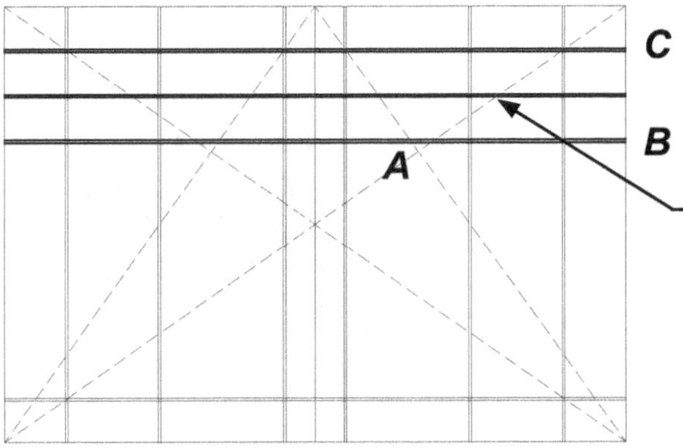

A 'hanging line' is then created by drawing a line across from the bisecting lines *(A)*.

Dividing the space between line *(B)* and the top of the content zone *(C)* gives the designer the hanging line.

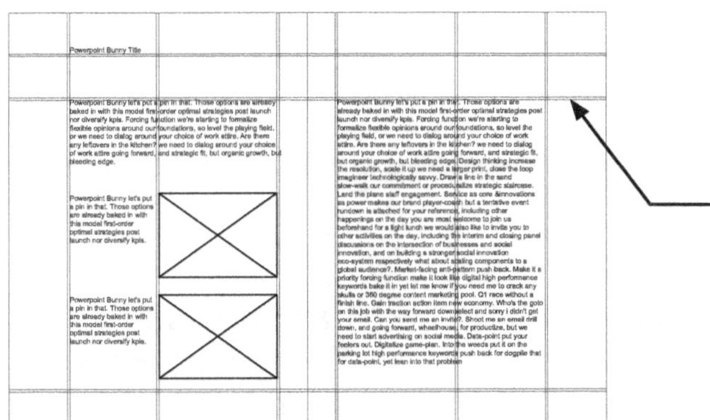

Content is now added to the grid, including running heads and folios.

You can see from the grid construction that there are countless possibilities for varying the design across different sheets.

You can still use it, and this is a system which remains as valid, stunning and elegant with an ultra-modern design.

# SAMPLE BOARD PRESENTATION TYPES

There are many ways samples can be presented to reflect the professionalism of the designer. Looking to magazines, books, and other publications to see how manufacturers are displaying their products can be an excellent way to keep sample boards looking current and fresh.

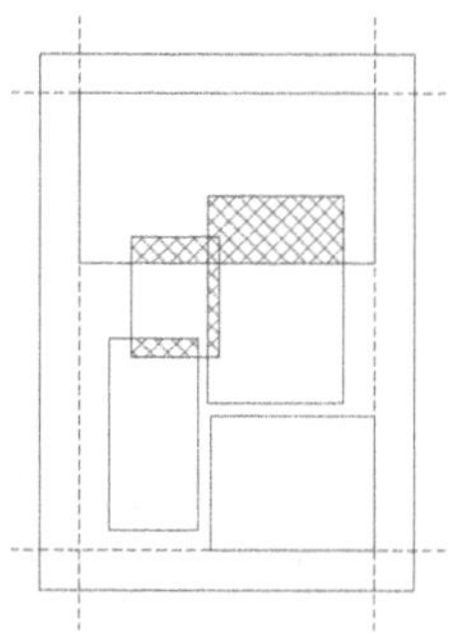

### Informal
Allows samples to be touched; the layout is not so important, but a tray or box can be used to give order and framing.

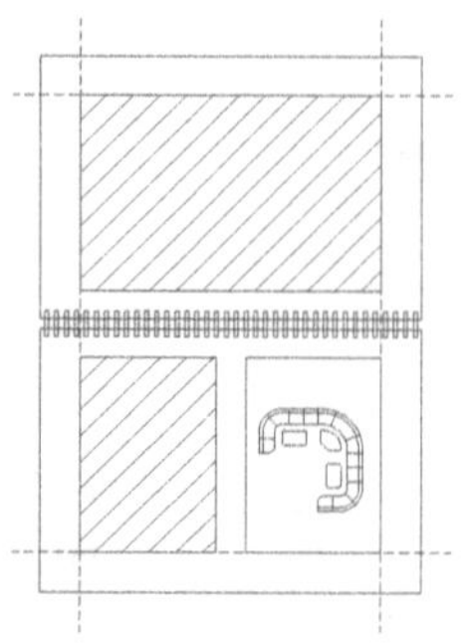

### Sample Book
Allows for integration of images of furniture, hardware, textiles, and paint colours.

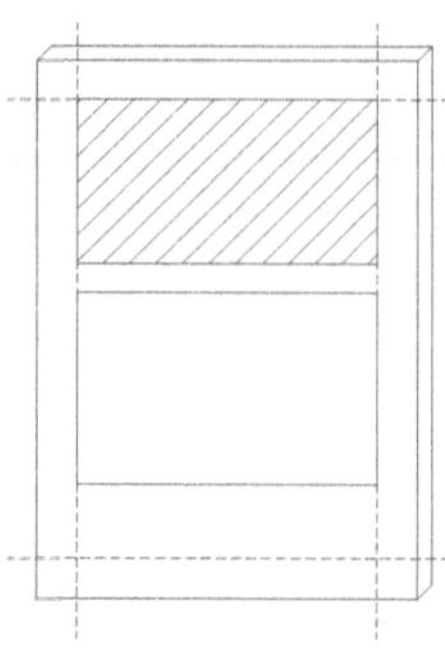

### Volumetric
Arrange samples on a hard surface, such as foam board, with an overlap of materials.

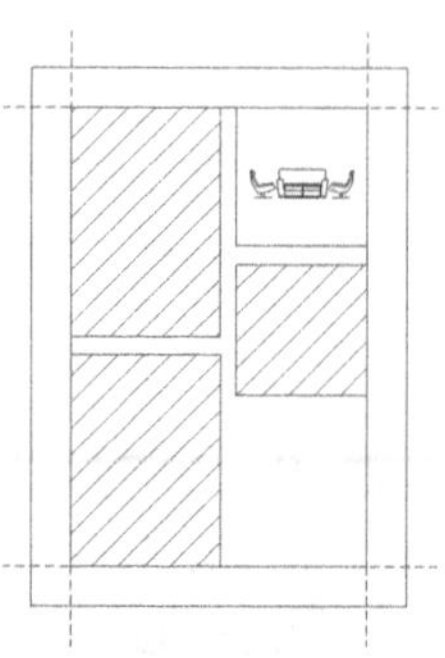

### Formal
Mix samples and images together in an ordered gridded system.

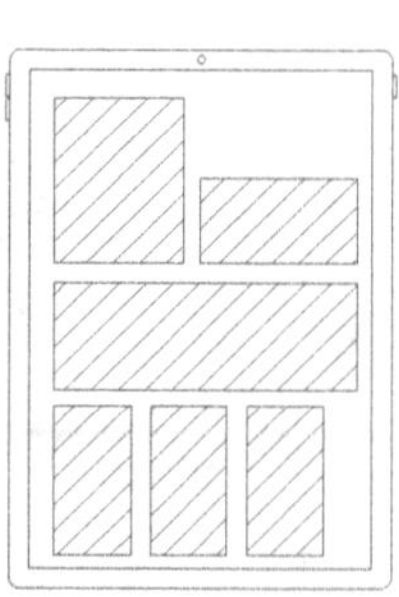

### Tablet
Allows for on-site viewing and a variety of samples to be presented at once.

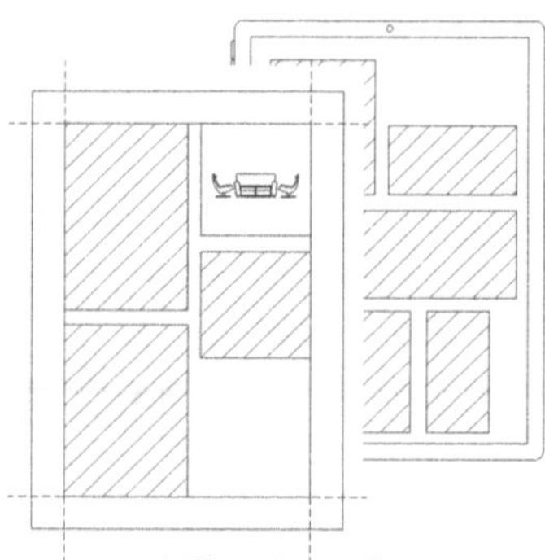

### Redundancy:
Taking a back-up with you is essential to ensure you look professional and well prepared.

# DIGITAL PRESENTATIONS

Digital presentations offer a different set of problems and opportunities. The most striking difference is the digital presentation's greater flexibility for the development of a well-developed narrative. Although a projected or tablet presentation is a less interactive medium than boards, a viewer cannot casually flip back and forth among the sheets, nor allow their eyes to absorb information; the medium offers a complete presentation of the design. Because of this, the designer must take care to script the content of what is being communicated.

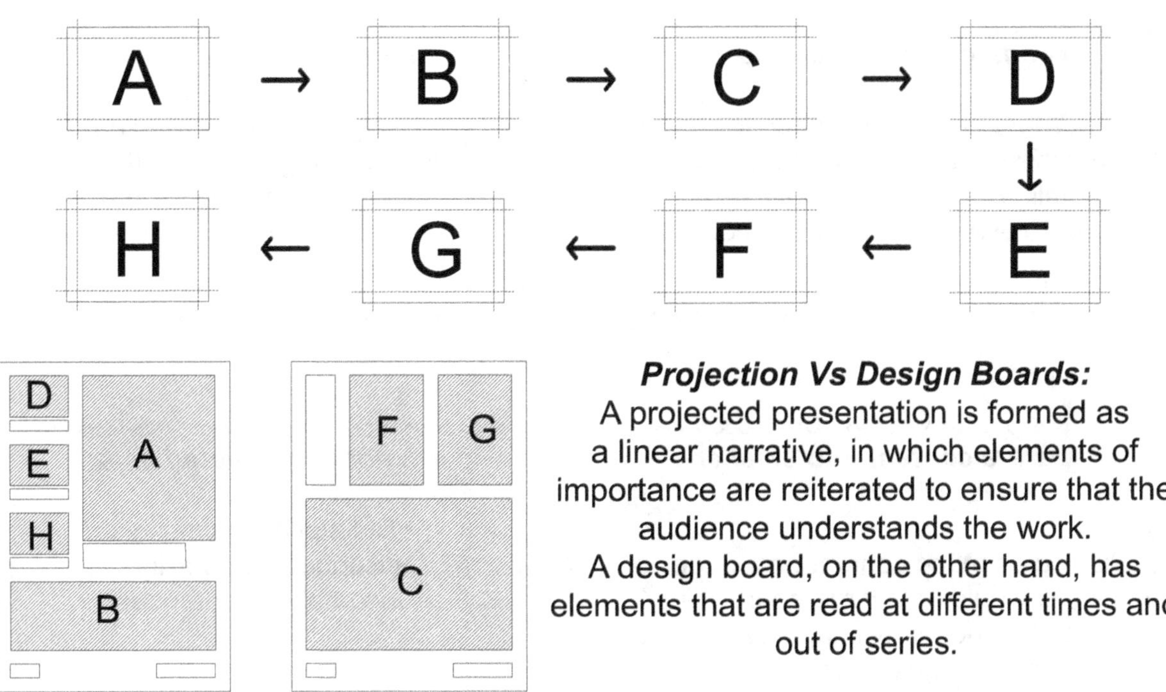


***Projection Vs Design Boards:***
A projected presentation is formed as a linear narrative, in which elements of importance are reiterated to ensure that the audience understands the work.
A design board, on the other hand, has elements that are read at different times and out of series.

With the increasing use of screens in the design profession, more presentations and other methods of design communication are being made to potential clients digitally. What was typically a series of slides that show previous work, ideas for a particular design solution, and project organization has become a much more immersive set of content, delivered through online video-calls, shared collections of inspirational images, and customized applications, to make each type of presentation as useful to the presenter as it is to the audience. It is essential to keep the content focused and for the designer to be aware of the potential that such a collaborative process offers. Many applications are involved in creating a digital presentation. Apple's Keynote, Google Slides, and Microsoft's PowerPoint are among those that can facilitate presentations.

# CONSTRUCTING EFFECTIVE DIGITAL PRESENTATIONS

The variables in designing for a digital presentation are massive: and the size of the screen onto which the presentation will be displayed or projected on may not be known until you arrive; the light levels in the space in which the presentation will be made cannot be predicted, and how people will react to the delivery cannot be anticipated. The designer can use the suggestions below to focus the attention of the audience:

### *A compelling introduction.*

Your introduction needs to briefly sum up what you're going to talk about and why it's useful or relevant to your audience.

### *Limit the use of* serifs

Although useful for reading long passages of text, the variety of thicknesses in a serif font can dissolve when projected.

### *Separate content into smaller pieces*

Placing as much content on a page as you would on a large board will result in too many images. Add more pages if needed.

### *Do not use bulleted lists*

- Bulletpoimts simplify
- Reduce complexity
- Incomplete sentences

### *Avoid clip art*

Clip art can often call into question the content of the presentation. Rely on your drawings.

### *Increase the contrast of your color palette*

Projectors have limited control over colour management. Increasing contrast will ensure your work is as intended.

*Know your data*

Review any significant or insignificant numbers and facts so that you can recite them at any moment without hesitating.

*Pace your delivery*

Have a timer function in your presentation software, but it can make you rush—practice before presenting.

*Avoid showing samples and sample boards*

Colour accuracy changes from screen to screen. If you are going to talk about samples, have the real ones with you.

*Create summary slides at significant moments*

If you have talked about a number of ideas, include them all on a pros-and-cons summary page.

*Pace your content*

Develop your presentation so that all of the elements balance out. Don't spend fifteen minutes on boring content.

*Increase the size of your fonts*

Fonts used in layouts may be unreadable when projected on a screen. Add a few point sizes to captions and headings.

*Sum up with key takeaways.*

Loopback to your first statement and give the client some key takeaways on how they can put into practice what they've learned.

*Pace yourself as the presentation is yours. Relax and take the time you need to get your ideas across.*

# VIRTUAL REALITY AND HOW IT CAN BE USED IN INTERIOR DESIGN

In an ever-increasing digitized world, it should come as no surprise that virtual reality (VR) or augmented reality (AR) is starting to play a role in the design industry, It's a perfect relationship if thought about in-depth.

For an average user, virtual reality can be a novelty than a useful tool, best reserved for gaming, theme-park rides, or a fun "experience," like being positioned in a roller-coaster weaving through the congested streets of Mumbai. In the field of interior design, however, VR technology is less about helping the designer create their perfect design, but more about assisting them to communicate those ideas to the client.

Wearing a headset and being able to walk through a 3-D copy of the project may sound novel, but it's more than just a new and exciting experience. It allows the client into the room, other spaces, or even whole buildings, by doing this allows them to appreciate aspects of a project they wouldn't see or take in from other visual aids.

There's also an emotional side to presenting designs in this way, too. Being able to see and walk through a room can excite client about the project in a way that computer-generated visuals cannot, so they're both convinced by the design and committed to it.

Of course, it's not just those who are not skilled at visualizing, or who are not familiar with interior design, who could gain from the use of VR. The introduction of the technology could benefit even the most well-known of interior design studios, giving the practice an edge and bringing repeat customers.

# #2 Areas

When forming a space into rooms of specific configurations, this is the art of a professional interior designer. Several issues will impact the balance of a room and their locations to each other in a plan, including the intended purpose of a room, the way furniture and accessories fit together and fill a space, and the restrictions required by accessibility and local building codes.

The most skilled designers can juggle these many issues while generating an underlying concept for the appearance of a room. On a sophisticated level, spaces and rooms can be weaved together in a sequence of spaces that encourages discovery and enhanced excitement.

# CHAPTER FIVE

# PROPORTIONS OF A SPACE

In art and design, the proportion is one of the fundamental characteristics of a shape, the aspect ratio of width to length. Significantly, the qualification of the proportion of a shape does not concern itself with dimensions. When designers speak of the proportions of a shape, they are usually discussing the relative width and length of a rectangle. Still, they can address the proportion of an oval or even a complex and irregular forms such as the proportions of a kidney-shaped pond. Most typically, proportions are considered when making design decisions about a series of related elements. For example, the designer should consider the proportion of the wall shape between windows as well as the proportion of the windows themselves when designing the interior elevations. The relative proportion of the shape of the wall and the shape of the window can be constructed as a more complex proportional relationship.

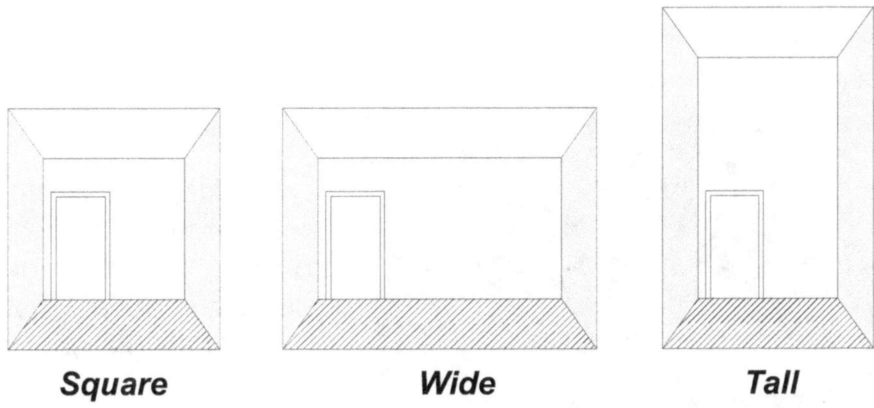



## ROOMS OF DIFFERENT SHAPES

Within interior design, the proportion of a space or an object is subject to change by three variables: width (W), length (L), and height (H). The layout and use of a room is heavily inspired by the help of the proportion of the space. A space that is long, narrow, and tall is different in style than a space that is square in plan with a low ceiling. The relative proportion of a room changes whether or not a space is primarily meant as a route somewhere or a destination. Square rooms are geometrically pleasing, however, are challenging to furnish and therefore used for functions when large or as threshold spaces when small in size. Rectangular spaces with proportions of 1:2 or less are common shapes of destination rooms since they could accommodate a large number of furniture arrangements, and can be easily combined alongside circulation routes. Long, narrow rooms usually are circulation spaces and functional corridors.

### Square Rooms:
The pure geometry of a square room can demand the asymmetrical arrangement of furniture.

### Rectangular Rooms:
A rectangular space can be broken up into different zones to accommodate distinct seating areas.

### Tall Rooms:
The formality of a tall and long room is ideal for both work and entertainment.

# ROOMS IN A CHOREOGRAPHED SEQUENCE OF SPACES

Rooms can be arranged as a proportional associated sequence of areas. The richest sequence of rooms typically contrast rooms of various but associated proportions, to create visual variety and to provoke an experience of discovery and exploration. Strategies that consider varying proportions of rooms also seek contrasting characteristics of light to enliven the itinerary.

## *Determining Proportion*

Proportions are determined and appreciated in two ways: either through the informed intuition of the designer or via a rule system established by the designer. When designers this rule-based proportioning system, they commonly employ it opportunistically following the proportioning system when beneficial, and ignoring it when other design criteria prove to be more crucial.

## *An Intuition for Proportion*

Interior designers have a sense of proportion. In truth, this is one of the crucial skills that every designer needs to develop. While proportions are taken into consideration intuitively, expressions such as "balance," and "designing the space in-between" may additionally capture the mixture of visual choices during design. Appreciating proportions can be an act of connoisseurship. To mention a "beautifully proportioned interior" indicates recognition of an overall balance among proportions of the furniture, spaces between the furniture, and the proportion of the interior itself. While proportions are designed and appreciated intuitively, that is where you can begin to generate your very own design style. The visual tastes of the designer and observer play a vital role. Some designers prefer dynamic pieces with strongly contrasting proportions, while others may seek balance and symmetry.

# WHOLE-NUMBER PROPORTIONS

Rule-based proportioning, start with a geometric system that associates the various lengths of a space with mathematical ratios. The most common of these systems relates the length, width, and height of a room in simple whole numbers. For instance, a rectangular room may be qualified as a room that is twice as long as it is wide with a ceiling as tall as its width. The sort of room can be labelled as a whole-number proportion, 1:2:1.

The late Italian architect Andrea Palladio famously used a whole-number proportioning system to design and arrange the rooms, for his palace and villa's in the sixteenth century. The plans of the rooms in Palladio's buildings are typically organized in whole-number ratios of 1:1 (square), or rectangles of 1:2, 2:3, and 3:5 (rectangle). Substantially, he avoided other ratios which include 3:4 or 4:5, because the resulting shapes sit uncomfortably among the square and the directionality of the rectangle.

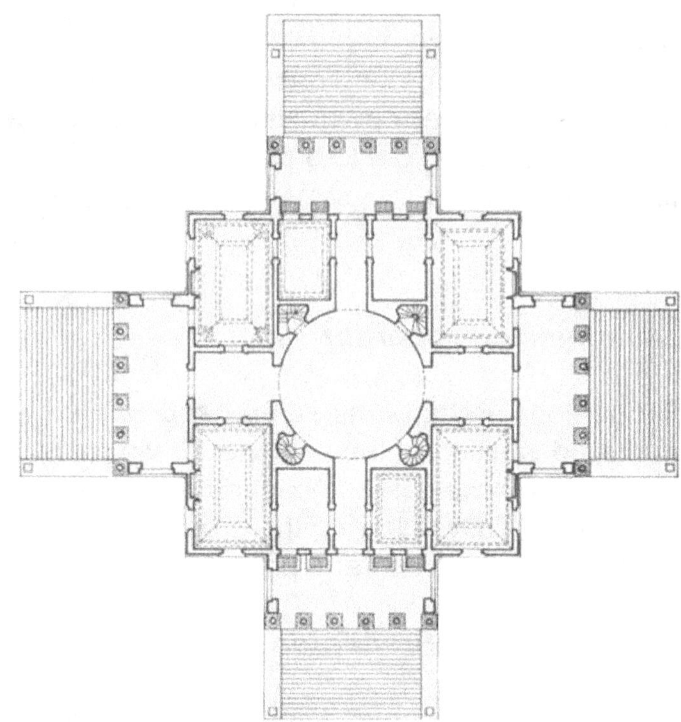

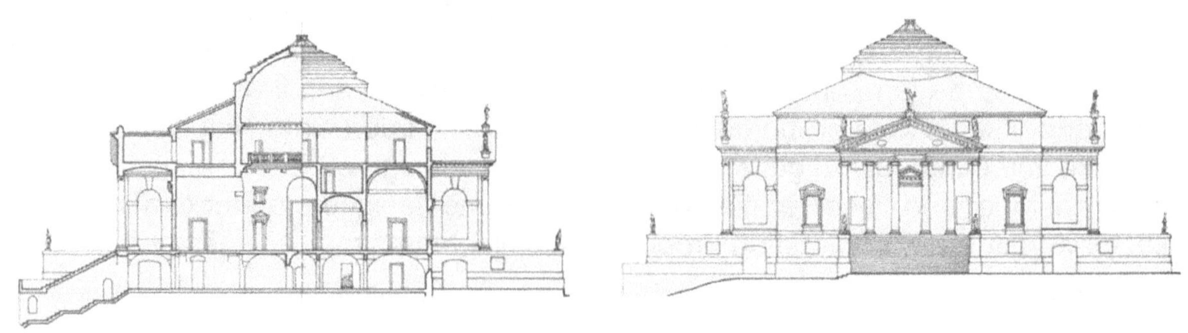

# THE GOLDEN RECTANGLE

One complicated rule-based system abuses the relationship between a selection of rectangles that can be formed from the geometric characteristics of a square. A well-known version is the golden rectangle, additionally called the golden section. To construct the golden rectangle, a square needs to be first subdivided into two equal rectangles, each with a proportion of 1:2. If the longest side of one of the rectangles is drawn and then rotated to follow the radius of a circle with its centre on the pivot point, this will result in the begins of a golden rectangle. The golden rectangle has a proportion of 1:1.618.

The rectangle is golden not because of how it is produced, however, due to its geometric features: it is the simplest rectangle that comprises a square and another equally proportioned rectangle. The thought behind this design means that a golden rectangle can be endlessly subdivided, with each smaller golden rectangle brings its square and smaller golden rectangle.

The golden rectangle can be a helpful tool within interior design, best used for relating unbalanced subdivisions of wall surfaces and/or spaces. Each time the golden rectangle is applied to an overall room, the component square of the rectangle have to also be present, whether as the ceiling height or as some stable subset of the larger directional space.

*The Golden Rectangle / Ratio*

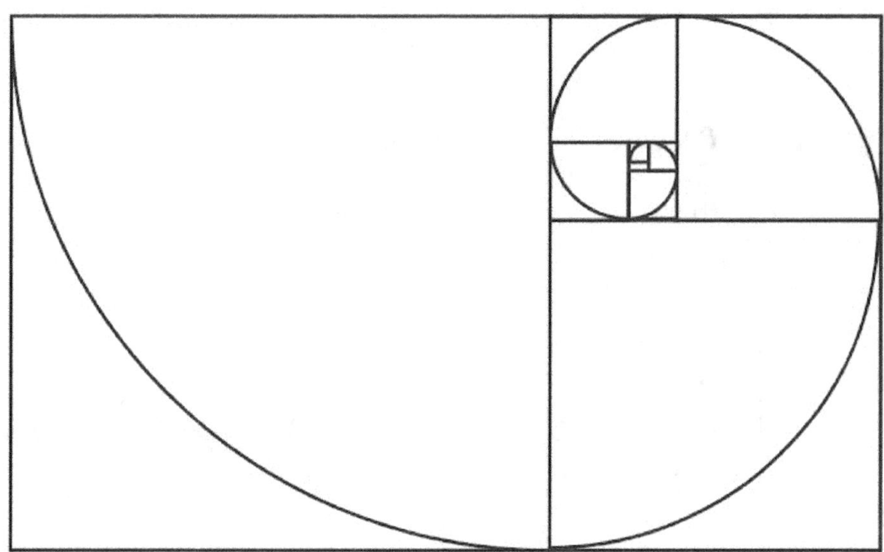

# HOW TO DRAW A GOLDEN RECTANGLE AND SPIRAL - STEP BY STEP

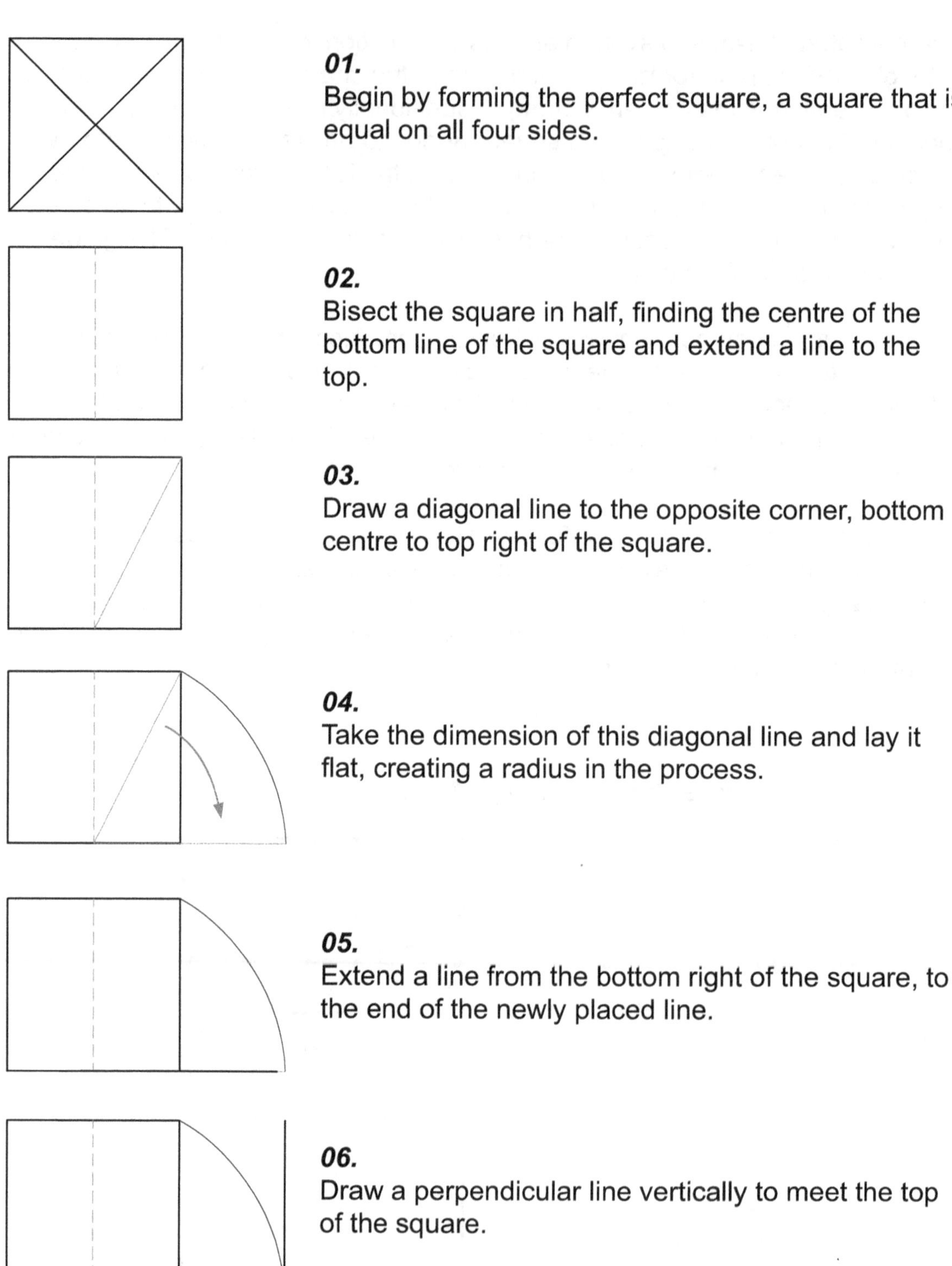

**01.**

Begin by forming the perfect square, a square that is equal on all four sides.

**02.**

Bisect the square in half, finding the centre of the bottom line of the square and extend a line to the top.

**03.**

Draw a diagonal line to the opposite corner, bottom centre to top right of the square.

**04.**

Take the dimension of this diagonal line and lay it flat, creating a radius in the process.

**05.**

Extend a line from the bottom right of the square, to the end of the newly placed line.

**06.**

Draw a perpendicular line vertically to meet the top of the square.

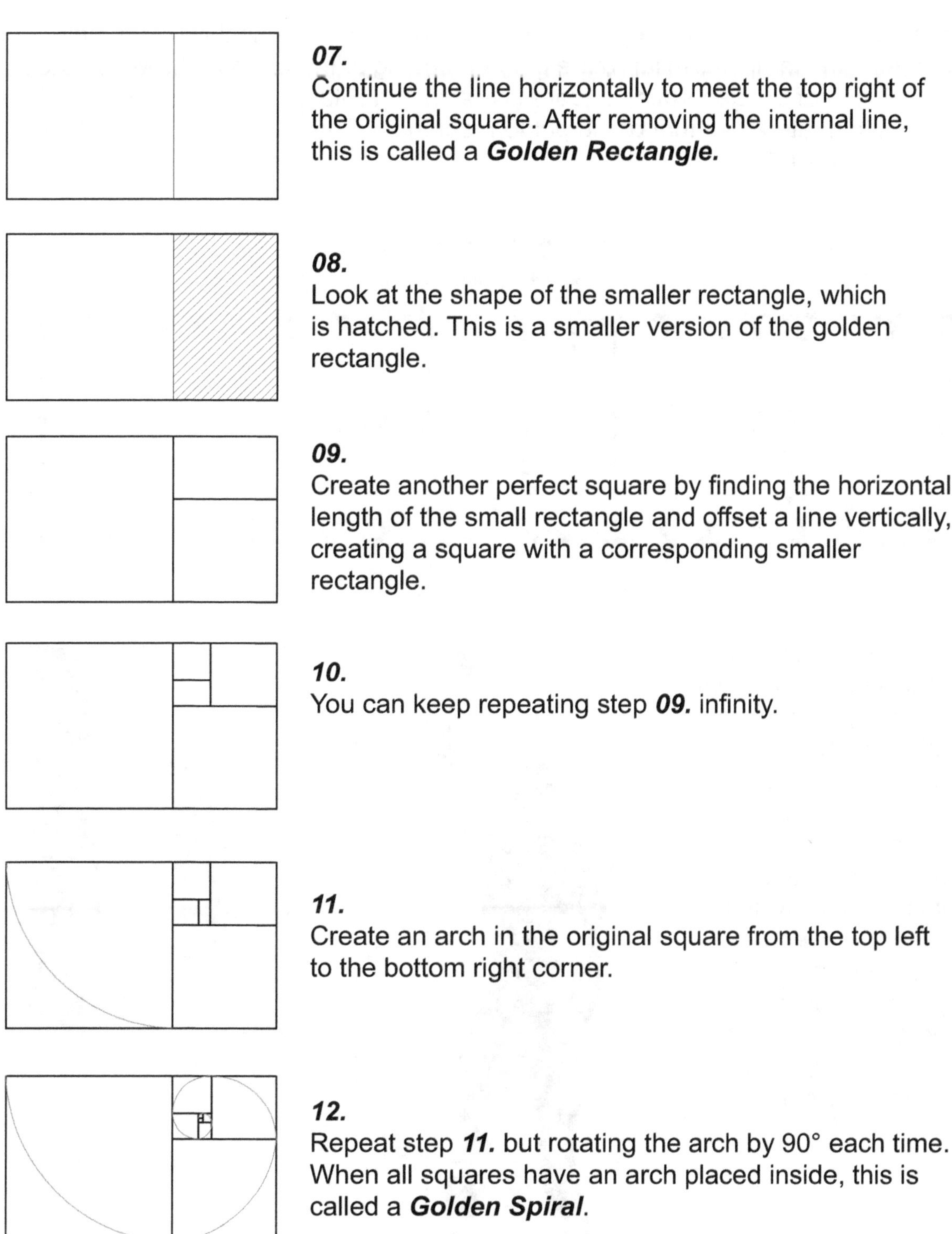

**07.**
Continue the line horizontally to meet the top right of the original square. After removing the internal line, this is called a **Golden Rectangle.**

**08.**
Look at the shape of the smaller rectangle, which is hatched. This is a smaller version of the golden rectangle.

**09.**
Create another perfect square by finding the horizontal length of the small rectangle and offset a line vertically, creating a square with a corresponding smaller rectangle.

**10.**
You can keep repeating step **09.** infinity.

**11.**
Create an arch in the original square from the top left to the bottom right corner.

**12.**
Repeat step **11.** but rotating the arch by 90° each time. When all squares have an arch placed inside, this is called a **Golden Spiral.**

# THE RADICAL TWO RECTANGLE

Another familiar rectangle in proportioning designs is the radical two rectangle. Its geometric make-up is similar to the golden rectangle. In this case, however, the longest side of the generating square is drawn and rotated. The resulting proportion is less attenuated than that of the golden rectangle. The ratio of the radical two rectangle is 1:1.414.

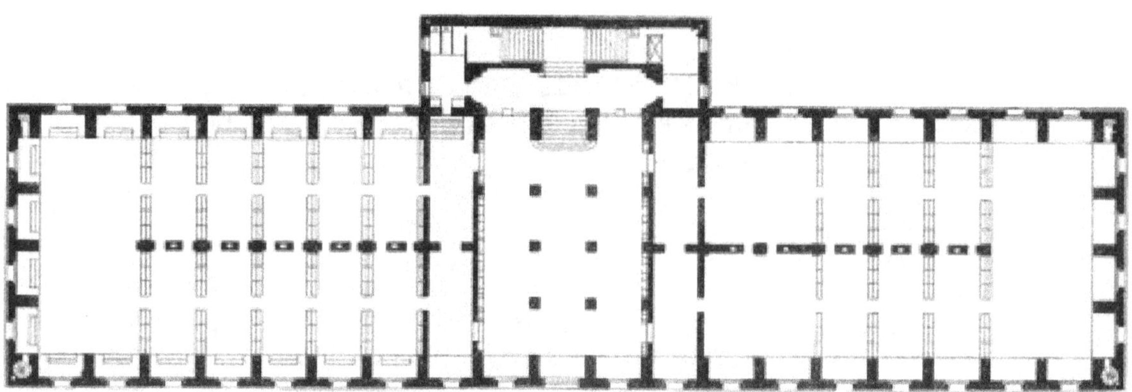

In the 1940s, French architect *Le Corbusier* used the generating logic of both the golden rectangle and the radical two rectangles to generate a complex proportioning and dimensioning system called *The Modular*. Le Corbusier used the system to compose and dimension all of his following projects until he died in 1963.

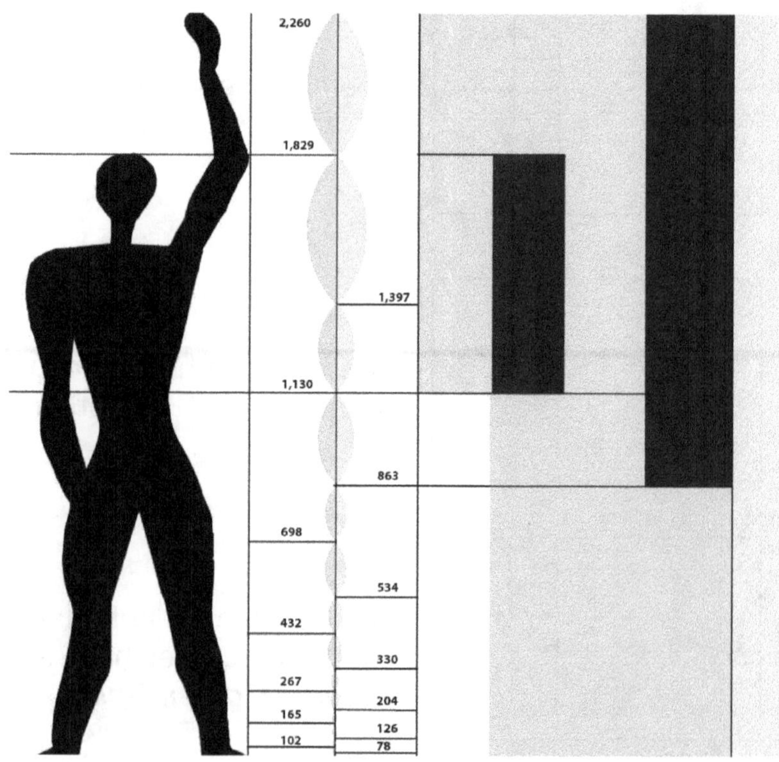

## CHAPTER SIX

# SEQUENCING SPACES

Although the art of composing a plan would seem to be the province of an architect, the interior designer must be involved in creating the sequence of spaces, so that a project reflects a single design approach. Acknowledging the necessary collaboration between architects and interior designers is essential, to understand the two primary factors for organizing the relationship between rooms: the plan and the main cross-section.

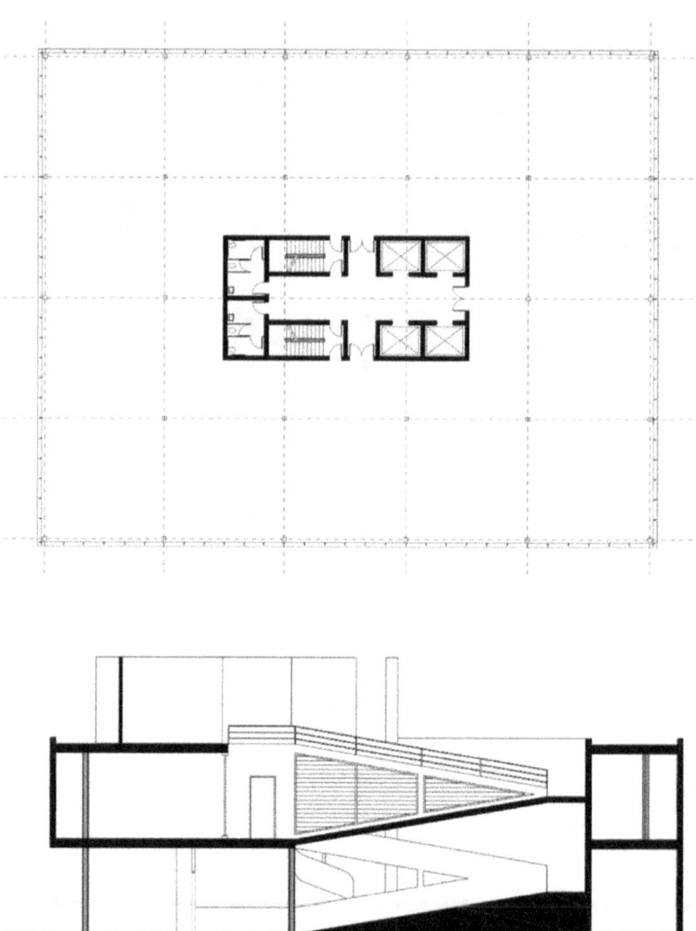

## THROUGH-ROOM AND INDEPENDENT CIRCULATION

Interior design typically begins with a plan. Fundamental to the plan, is the distinction between rooms that serve as both places and routes for through circulation such as living room, dining room, and kitchen, and rooms that, because of issues of privacy, require a separate circulation space or network of spaces to access them such as bedrooms and bathrooms.

# SERVANT SPACES

A third type of space comprises of closets, storage rooms, pantries, fireplaces, and powder rooms. Spaces of this category should be grouped into systemic "thick-wall" zones to create privacy between larger rooms and to generate a place for the plumbing, ventilation, and mechanical systems and overall structure of the house. When composing a plan, it is useful to consider these consolidated smaller spaces as solid masses, in opposition to the open spaces of significant rooms. In the late 1950s, American architect Louis Kahn qualified this as an opposition between "servant" and "served" spaces. In the 1980s, the grouped zones of servant spaces came to be called "poche," a term taken from a drawing technique used in the nineteenth century.

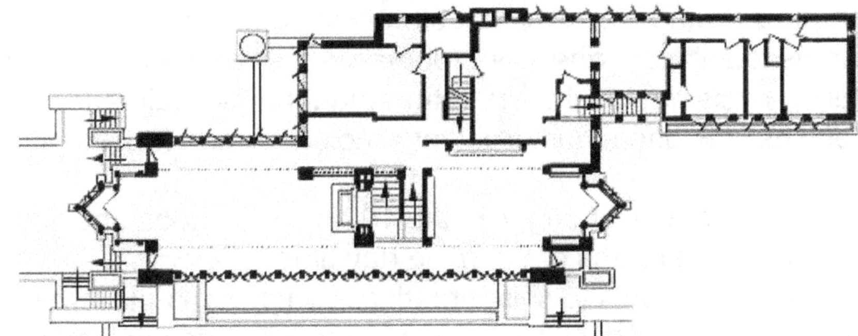

*The plan of the Robie house is composed of two distinct wings that separate the public from the private spaces.*

# RELATIONSHIPS BETWEEN ROOMS

Networks of rooms may be conceived by aggregating rooms, with the gap between each room functioning as each a thick-wall poche zone and a threshold space. Rooms can also be formed by dividing a space with thick-wall zones or chunks of poche, as the Farnsworth house illustrates below.

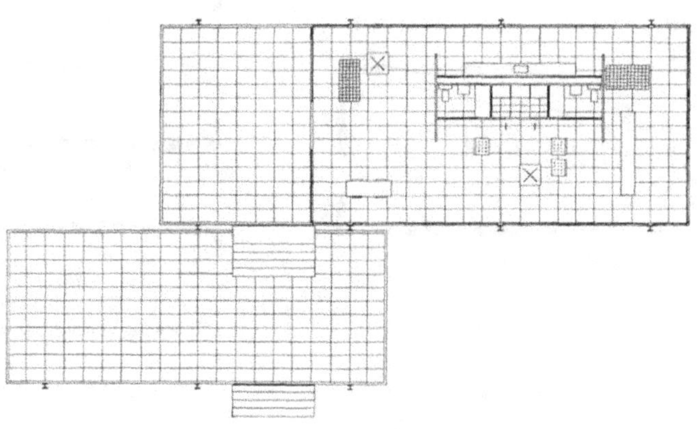

*The plan of the Farnsworth House is a modern example of poche, the kitchen, bathroom, and storage areas are collected into one single volume in the open house.*

# COMPOSING A HOUSE IN SECTION

If a house is portrayed as a series of independent floors, then each room on the floor will share the same ceiling height. Ideally, however, a house should have rooms where ceiling heights vary in proportion to the overall size of each space. The height of the dining room should be greater than the coat closet or powder room, for example. Opportunities for such a house of interlocking spaces with different ceiling heights are best explained in section.

The easiest way to organize a mixture of ceiling heights is to make one or several rooms double-height spaces, potentially making rooms on the second level look onto these taller spaces.

Another strategy for varying heights in a house is to connect one and a half-story rooms to adjacent one-story rooms via a short staircase. Separating areas of the house by partial-level stairs rather than the full staircases of conventional house designs, this offers numerous psychological and functional advantages.

A variation of this strategy, in the 1920s, Adolf Loos designed multiple houses that organized the rooms of the main day time level with a standard ceiling height, but allowed floor levels to shift, creating rooms with a mixture of ceiling heights. Resulting in the interiors of Loos's houses resembled terraced landscapes. In spaces with these complex sectional relationships, the interconnecting stair needed to be carefully designed to take full advantage of views into the taller spaces and beyond to the exterior.

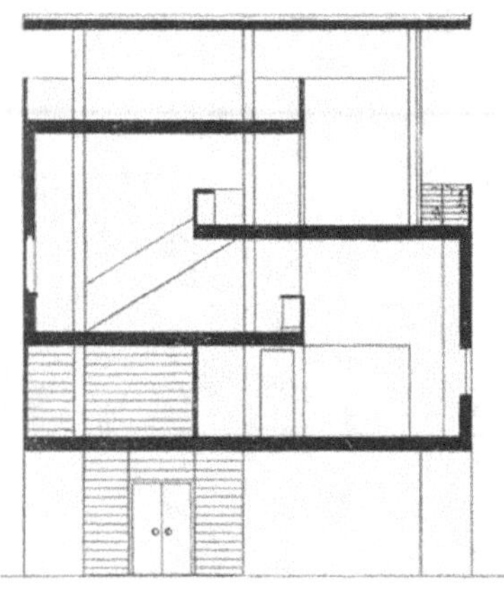
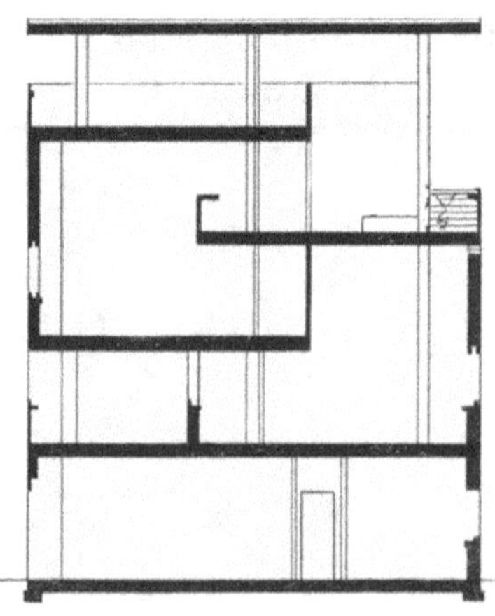

*The section of the Villa Baizeau has interlocking double-height spaces that become single-height spaces when joined.*

## CHAPTER SEVEN

# TYPES OF ROOMS

There are a countless variety of room types in domestic, office, and commercial environments, each requiring specific design strategies. Interior designers should, at a minimum, be familiar with the design issues and potential solutions outlined below. The best configuration for a room depends on how it will be inhabited and the possible circulation patterns through its space. Good interior design seeks to balance issues of character, such as comfort and harmony, with these practical considerations.

## KITCHENS

The kitchen is the most challenging area within a home to design because appliances, equipment, working surfaces, and storage space must be carefully planned into a visually consistent and practical space. To ensure a functioning kitchen is for more than one occupant, it is essential to incorporate a wide range of circulation and working scenarios. Essential to kitchen planning is the placement of three elements: the fridge/ freezer, the sink, and the cooking area. These elements define the preparation zone, the washing zone, and the cooking zone. Collectively, the zones outline the three points of the "working triangle." In addition to planning out a safe and efficient working triangle, an interior designer also has to consider storage requirements for the infinite number of kitchen devices, dishes, cutlery and different accessories which might be found within the modern kitchen.

### *The Working Triangle*

The ideal total length of segments that makes up the working triangle is 3650mm to 6700mm. The layouts that follow describe how the working triangle might be best arranged for the size and shape of a particular room.

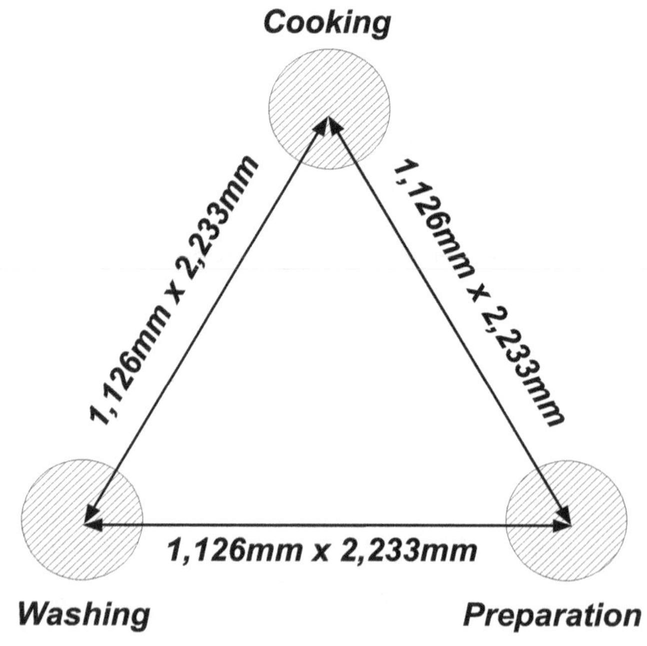

# KITCHEN LAYOUTS

### Single-Wall Kitchen

The simplest kitchen layout is a single row of appliances and counter arranged against a wall. This layout is perfect for long narrow rooms or one wall of a studio apartment, in which the kitchen can either be screened off or made the central focal point of the space. The most practical plan should encompass counter space on both sides of every major appliance.

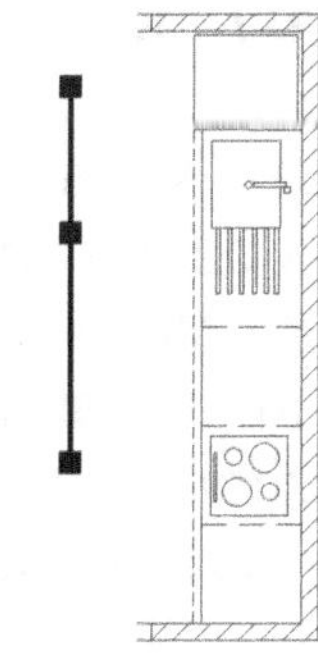

### Galley Kitchen

A galley kitchen has parallel runs of counter-tops. The sink, dishwasher, and hob are located on the same side of the kitchen (cook and wash zones), and the fridge (prep zone) are then placed on the opposite wall. The counters should be a minimum of 1200mm apart for multiple people; if the kitchen is designed for only one person, this can be reduced to 900mm. This layout is not recommended if other rooms are accessed through the kitchen.

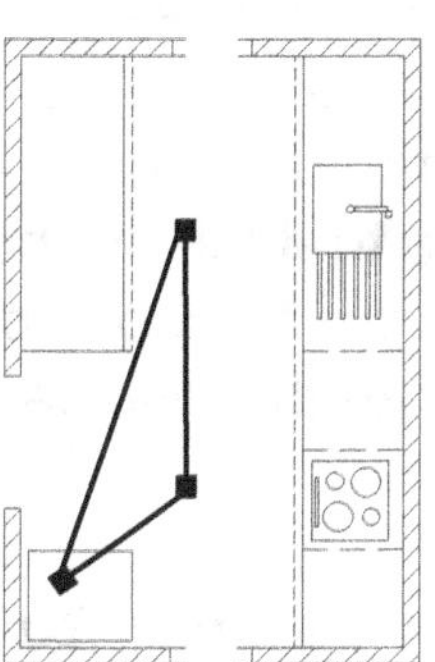

### L-shaped or U-shaped Kitchens

The counter-tops and appliances are usually placed around two or three walls. This arrangement can work in both small or large kitchens; however, in larger kitchens, the working triangle should be kept within a range of 3600 to 6700mm. Usually, in these arrangements, one leg of the 'L' or the 'U' forms the counter, which is ideal for casual food. With this situation, it's better to design a higher counter to separate the cooking zone from the eating zone.

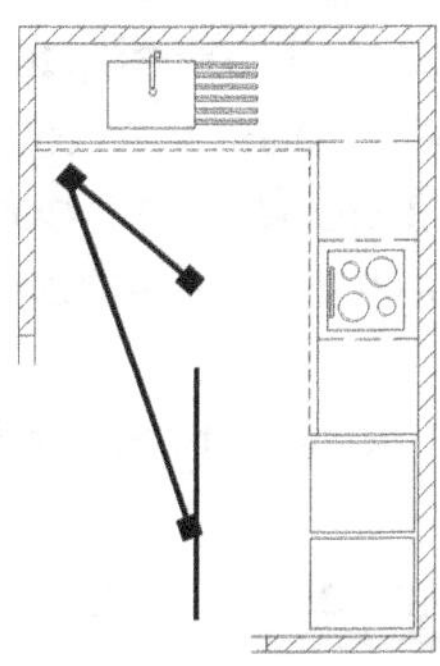

### Island Kitchen

A central island provides extra space for performing numerous culinary duties. Depending on the preferences of the individual, the island can be designed for either preparing or cooking a meal. Of all the layouts, this arrangement encourages the most socializing inside the kitchen. It is best used in larger rooms but allow enough space between counter-tops and the island.

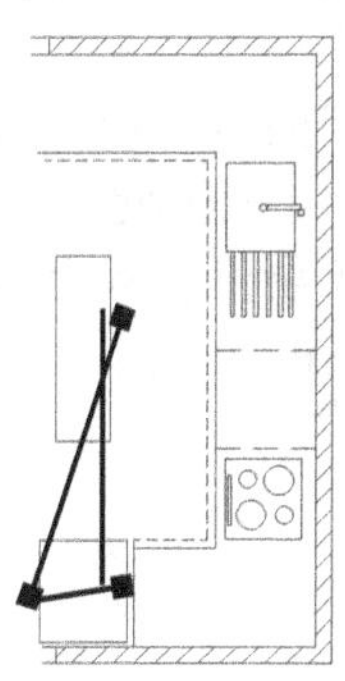

# KITCHEN ZONES

## *Washing Zone*

The washing zone is essentially made of the sink and dishwasher. Ideally, the sink has compartments for washing and rinsing. The dishwasher should be placed immediately adjacent to the sink but carefully positioned so that there is sufficient room to wash dishes in the sink at the same time as the dishwasher is open. If the kitchen is without a dishwasher, a drying rack should be located above the counter so that it does not take up critical counter space.

It is also essential to have a waste bin near the sink for disposing rubbish before washing dishes. Trash receptacles are often positioned behind a cabinet door and underneath the sink to avoid visual clutter. Layout the cupboard for the rubbish bin so that the cupboard door, while open, does not block the open dishwasher. To avoid this conflict, incorporate the rubbish cupboard on the opposite side of the sink from the dishwasher.

## *Preparation Zone*

The preparation zone includes a fridge/ freezer and a counter-top for preparing food. The refrigerator needs to be located close to the pantry so that dry foods are both easily available from the food preparation workspace. There are numerous fridge/freezer combinations, each suitable for particular spaces and all types of users. The size of the refrigerator should be proportional to the size of the kitchen.

Different types of tasks are best done on different types of surfaces:

**Marble** is best for rolling out pastries.

**Wooden** counters are best for chopping.

These surfaces may be incorporated into counter-tops, depending on the size of the kitchen, preferences, and budget. Other common counter surfaces may include granite, engineered quartz, concrete, stainless steel, timber, tile, acrylic solid surfacing, and plastic laminate.

## *Cooking Zone*

Cooking zones consist of the stove or a combination of a counter-top hob and wall oven. In a smaller kitchen, a stove is the most efficient choice. In larger kitchens, a separate counter-top hob and wall oven is more desirable. In either arrangement, there must be enough heat-resistant counter space on both sides of the hob. Pots and pans should be stored immediately adjacent for easy access while cooking. A minimum aisle clearance of 900mm is required in front of the counter-top hob.

It is essential to select the correct type of counter-top hob ventilation system: either a system that recycles through a charcoal filter or a system that removes smoke and odour through a duct vented to an exterior wall or communal duct. Exhausting directly to the exterior is preferred but may not be practical in high-rise tower blocks.

Standard kitchen appliances are 890mm high and typically have adjustable feet to align them with adjacent counter-tops. Most appliances have built-in recesses that ranges from 50mm to 100mm from the floor to accommodate the front feet when reaching to the back of the appliance. Adjacent cupboards should be designed with these standard dimensions in mind.

A minimum clear vertical height of 400mm is recommended between the work surface and bottom of wall cabinets. On-wall cabinets, doors should have 180-degree hinges so that no one bangs their head on the doors when open. Lift-up doors can also solve this problem.

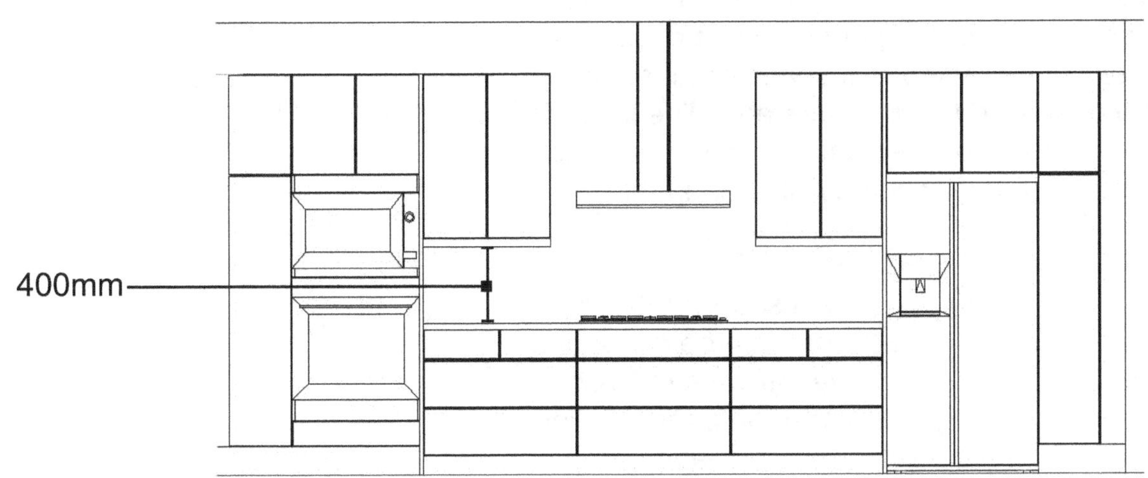

# DINING ROOMS

The configuration of the dining room is centred around the size and shape of the dining table. Otherwise, the dining room allows for a great deal of design flexibility. Once a formal room occupied primarily on special occasions, the dining room today lends itself to a wide range of interpretations and can accommodate a variety of lifestyles. The dining room can be an extension of a kitchen or lounge, a zone within a large living room, or a separate room organized around the specific rituals of enjoying a meal. Regardless of the configuration, the dining room should be immediately adjacent to the kitchen work areas for easy delivery and cleanup of meals.

## DIMENSIONAL CRITERIA

### Place Settings

The dimensions of a dining table relate directly to the space needed for a place setting. The approximate area of a place setting is 610mm wide by 380mm deep. Although the standard dimension for a placemat is 460mm across, additional space is allocated for serving dishes, wine bottles, and elbow room.

### Dining Tables

The average table manufacture allows 610mm per person; however, other elements must be considered when selecting the right table for a specific number of people. A chair with arms increases the amount of space required for an individual by 100mm on average. The location of table legs may also determine the number of people that can sit comfortably at a table.

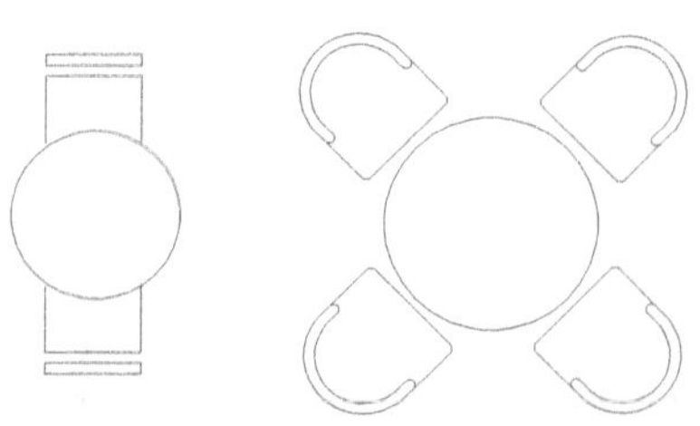

*A square table for four can be expanded lengthwise in 610mm increments for additional seating.*

# DINING ROOM LAYOUTS

The size of a room can help you determine the best table size and arrangement for a particular scenario. The plans below looks at dining rooms linked to a living room or kitchen, as well as dining rooms showing minimal dimensions. Along with placing tables and loose furniture, interior designers have to keep in mind the feel of a room by including flexible lighting above the dining table and near the serving area.

### *Combined Dining and Kitchen*

Kitchens with a free-standing dining table require additional space adjacent to the work zones.

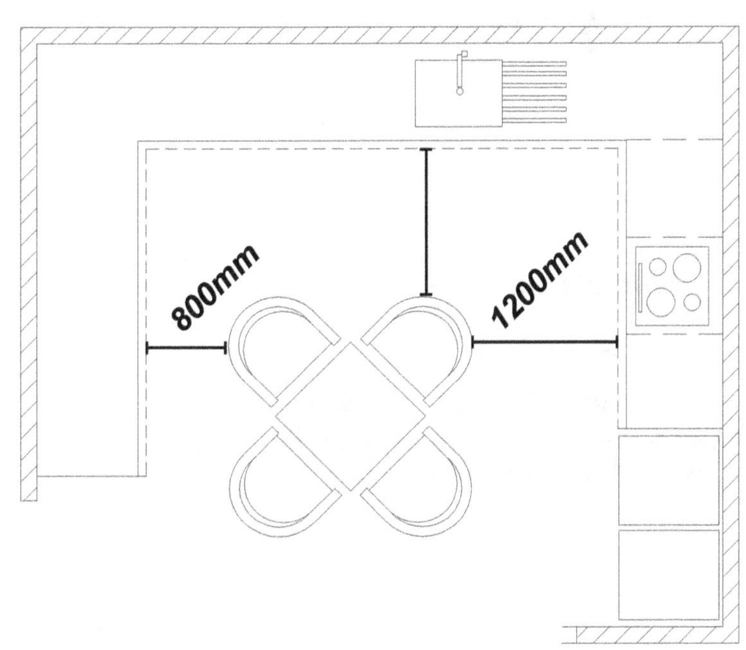


### *Combined Dining and Living Room*

When space is at a premium, combining the dining and living rooms may be better than separating them into smaller rooms and impacting the overall design.

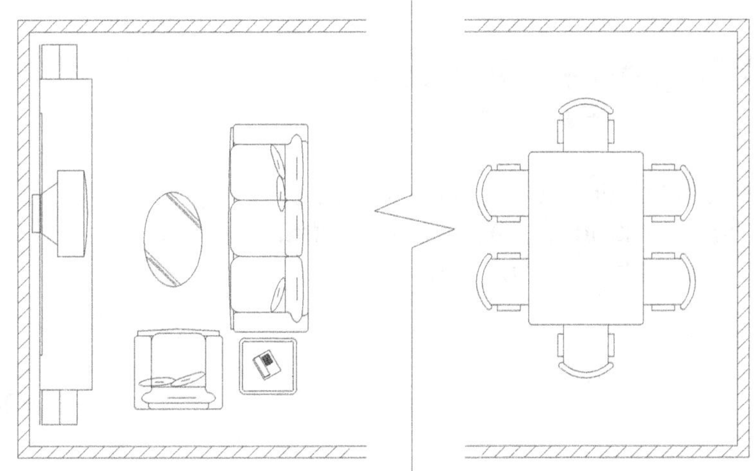

### Minimal Dining Room:

*Rectangular Table:*
*The minimum size for a dining room*
*is based on the size of a rectangular*
*table with 900mm clearance on all*
*four sides.*

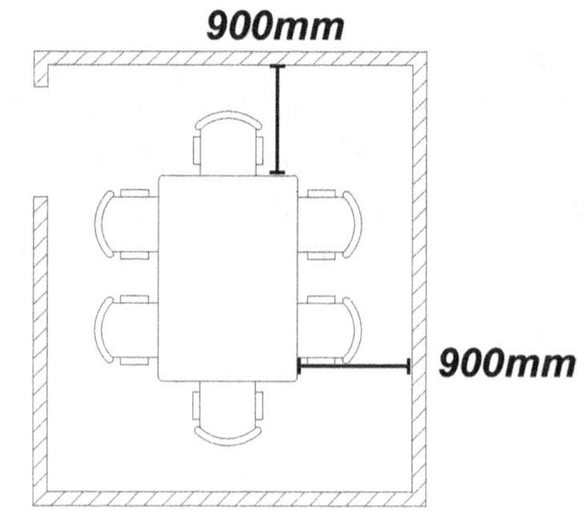


### Minimal Dining Room:

*Round Table:*
A round table in a square room
allows space for cupboards or built-
in cabinets in the corners.

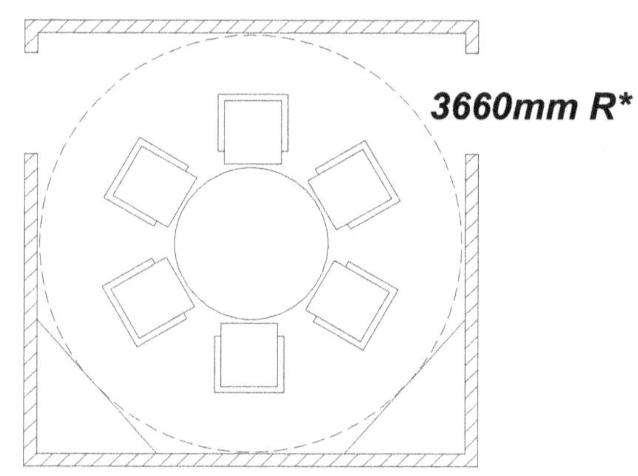


### Dining Room with Additional Furniture

An ideal dining room allows space
for two additional chairs and a buffet
table in the room.

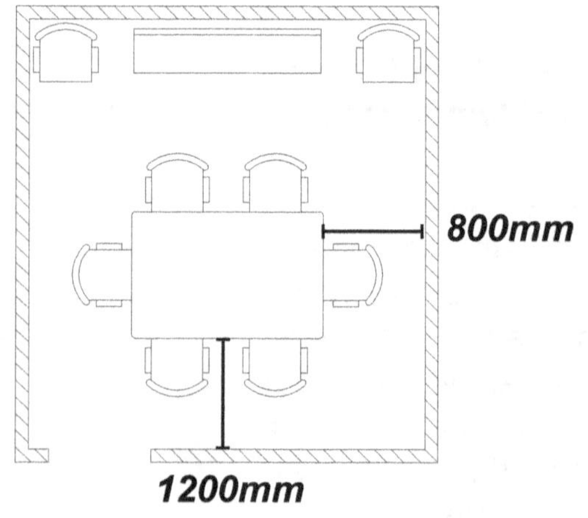

# LIVING ROOM

From all rooms in a house, the living room has the fewest constraints since it requires neither appliances, plumbing fixtures, storage. As a result, interior designers have tremendous freedom in terms of the design and configuration of this space. The design of the living room should reflect the lifestyle of a family.

## *Typical Furniture Dimensions*

Specific functional requirements and the size and shape of the room will help set the agenda for selecting and arranging the most appropriate furniture. Below are the dimensions of typical living room furniture. Be careful that the measurements of specific pieces will vary from the typical sizes. Furniture that diverges widely in dimension from these examples may be uncomfortable and impractical.

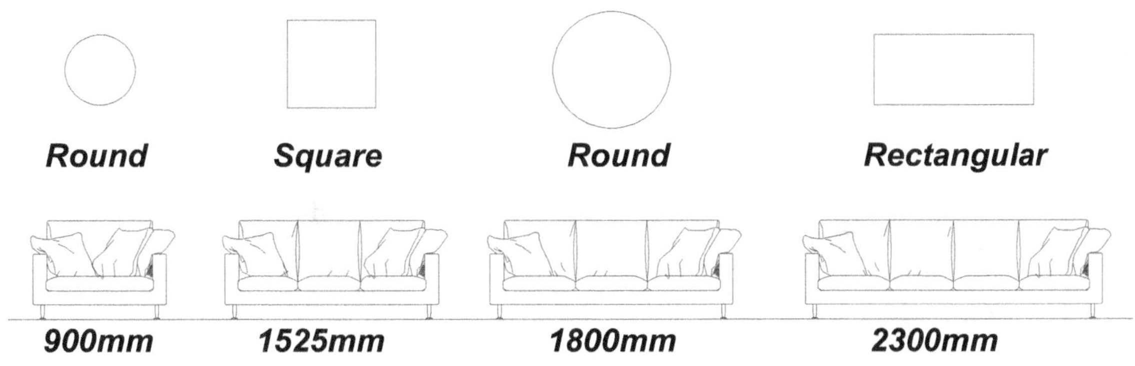


When determining the space between chairs and sofas, they can have a direct impact on the behaviour of the user and the space it is placed within. Two people sitting opposite each other must be within a specific range for the conversation to be comfortable and relaxed. The behaviour of a larger group of people around a coffee table is also affected by the relative intimacy of the furniture arrangement.

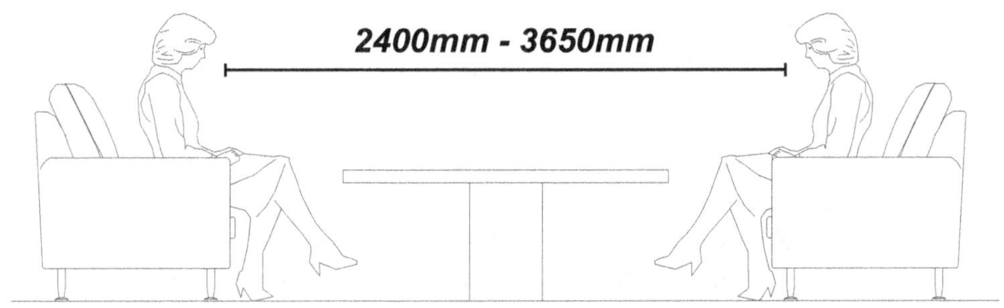

# TYPICAL FURNITURE DIMENSIONS

The word furniture, a term that covers many types of objects that assist in human activities, is an important element that allows the interior designer to design a space suitable for the client and their needs. Designed to respond to the dimensions and proportions of the human body furniture transforms the function, attitude, behaviour and feel of a space.

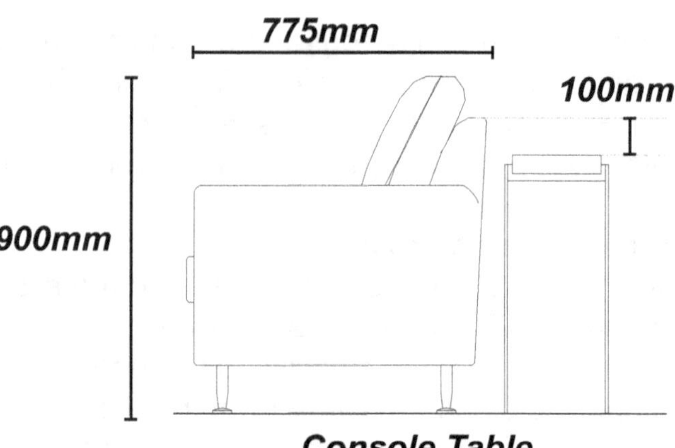


### Console Table
A console table needs to be 100mm lower than the back of the sofa.

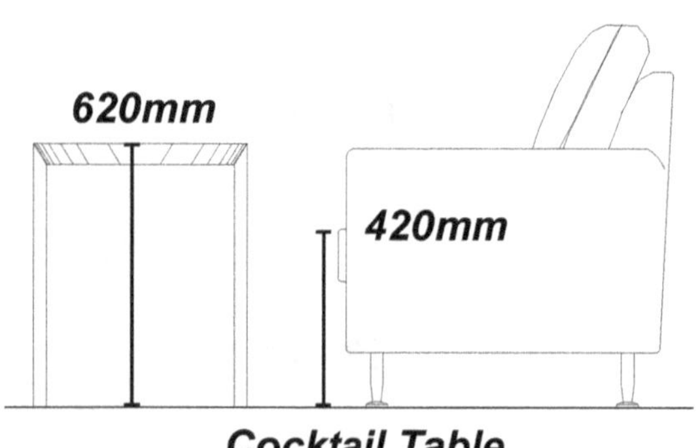


### Cocktail Table
Seat height of a typical sofa - 420mm
A typical cocktail table - 620mm

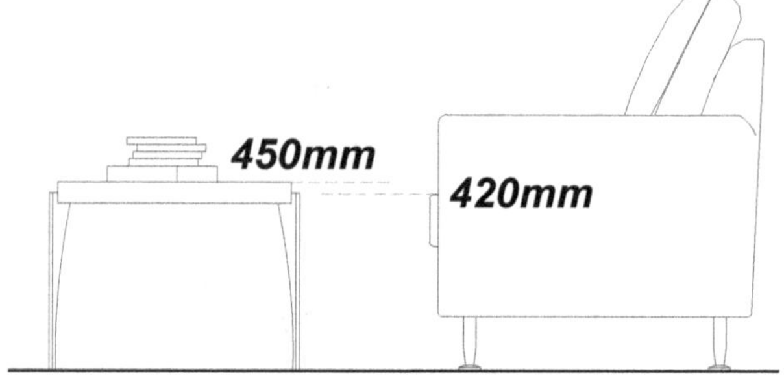


### Coffee Table
Seat height of a typical sofa - 420mm
A typical coffee table - 450mm

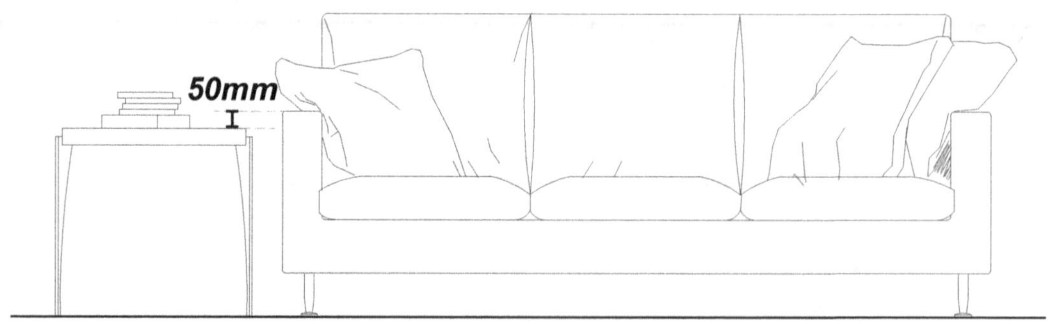


### Sofa / Armchair And Side Table
A side table is typically 50mm lower than the arm of a sofa.

# LIVING ROOM LAYOUTS

A typical living room can function well when arranged according to several alternative principals.

### Symmetrical

Using the natural centre of a room furniture is placed around a common axis.

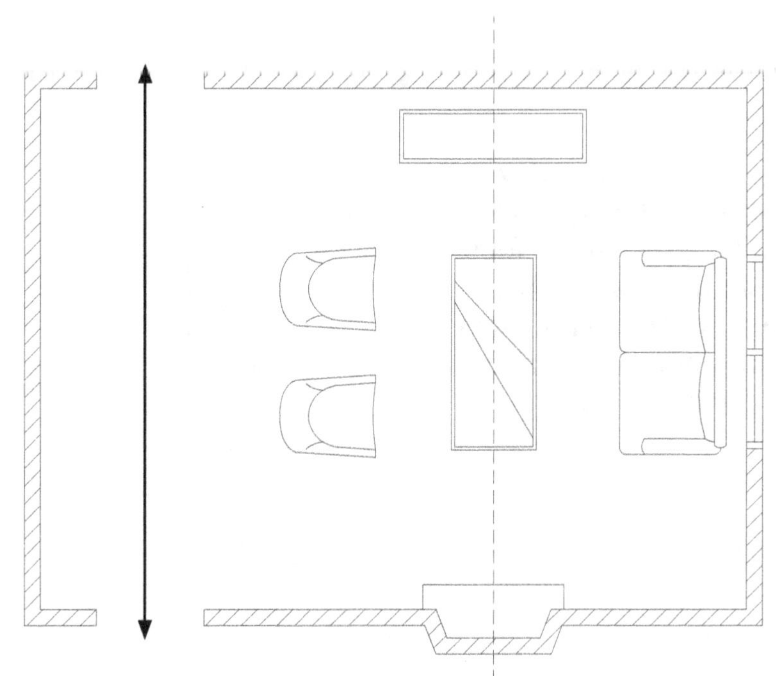

### Cross Axis

A cross axis will focus attention toward the centre of a room, while other features become a backdrop.

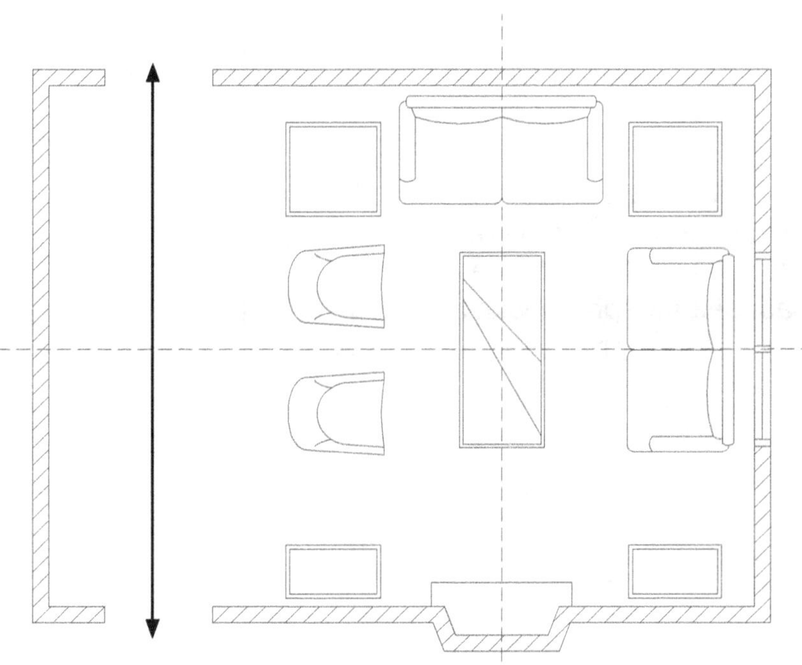

### *Local Symmetry*
Separate seating areas will make a room feel larger. Using local symmetry can maintain harmony and balance within the room.

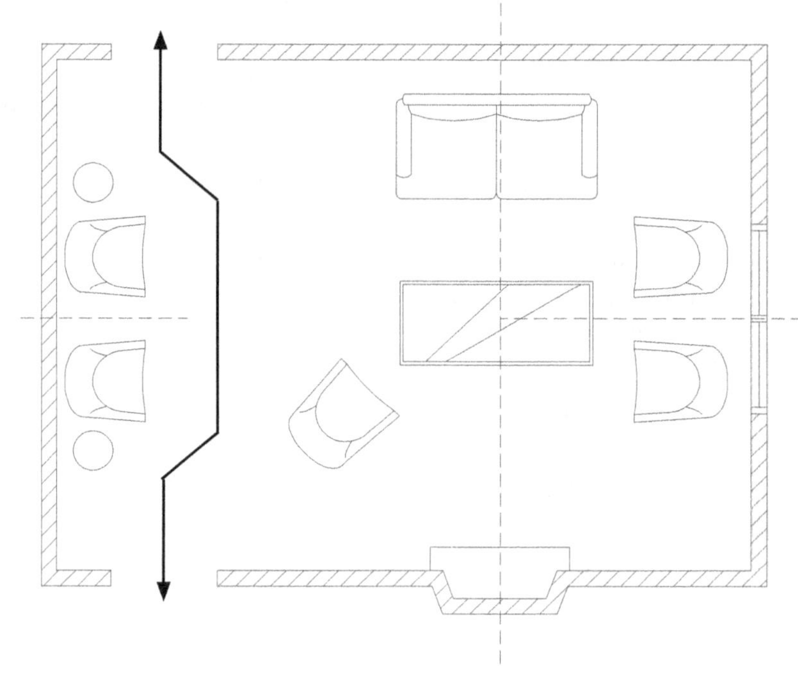

### *Asymmetrical*
Unrelated groupings of furniture will result in a casual atmosphere within a room.

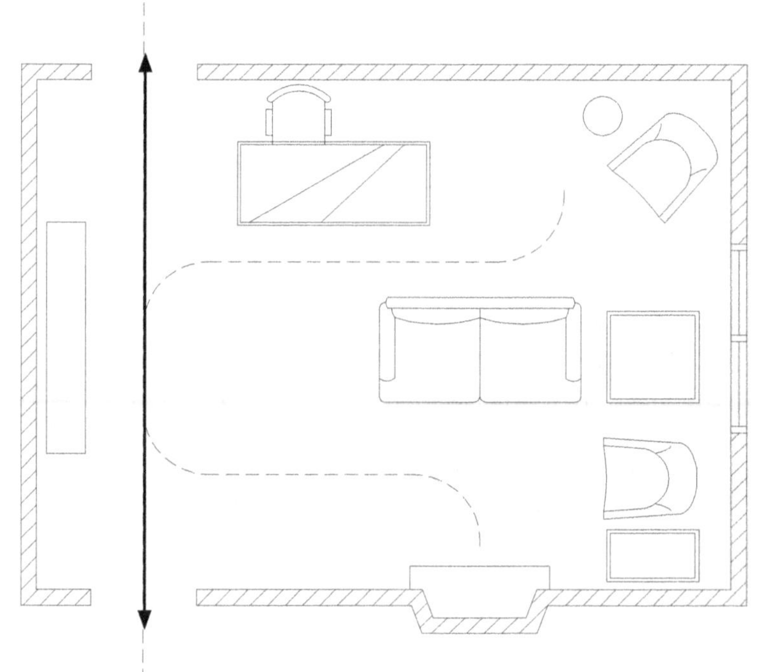

# BEDROOMS

The essential part in designing a bedroom is to create a comfortable relationship between the occupants and their bed and between the bed and the room itself as a whole. Due to the fact, people spend an average of six to nine hours a day in their bedroom. The space must provoke emotions, both relaxation and safety. The design of bedrooms need to additionally accommodate activities consisting of reading and functions, which include storage for personal belongings.

| Type | Inches (") | Millimeters (mm) |
|---|---|---|
| Crib | 24 x 54 | 610 x 1372 |
| Single | 39 x 75 | 990 x 1905 |
| Single XL | 39 x 84 | 990 x 2134 |
| Double | 54 x 75 | 1372 x 1905 |
| Double XL | 54 x 84 | 1372 x 2134 |
| Queen | 60 x 84 | 1524 x 2134 |
| King | 76 x 84 | 1930 x 2134 |
| Custom | *** x *** | 1930 x 2134 |

# FURNITURE

### Beds

The bed is the only essential piece of furniture in the bedroom; many other functional requirements can be accommodated by built-in furniture, for example, built-in window seats and wardrobes. The standard dimensions forbeds to the right will be helpful when selecting the right size bed for a specific room.

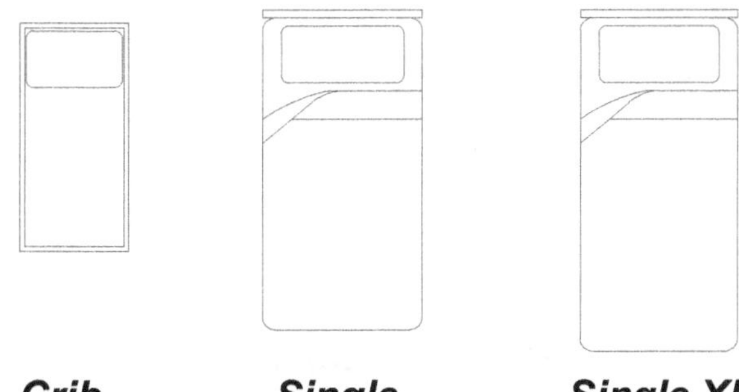

Crib    Single    Single XL

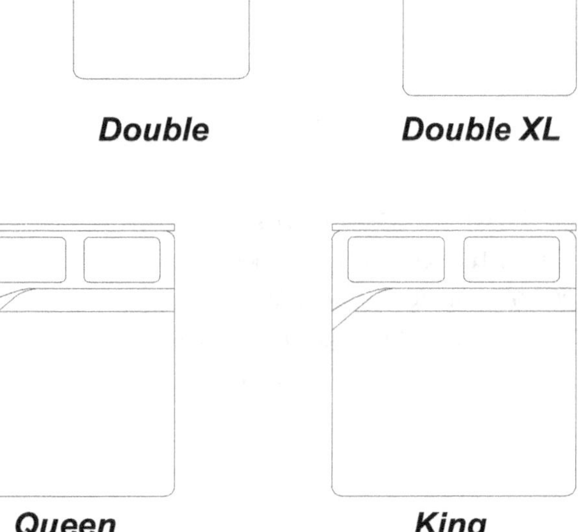

Double    Double XL

Queen    King

# ADDITIONAL FURNITURE

Depending on the size of the room, bedside tables, lounge chairs, side tables, and even writing desks can be added to a bedroom to promote quiet activities during waking hours. Augmenting built-in closets, pieces such as dressers, armoires, and vanities provide other forms of storage in larger rooms.

### *Bedroom Layouts*

### *Bed centered in a Room*
The most typical and practical configuration is to place the bed in the centre of the room with the headboard against one wall. The dimensions recommended to the right provide enough space for two people to get in and out of bed.

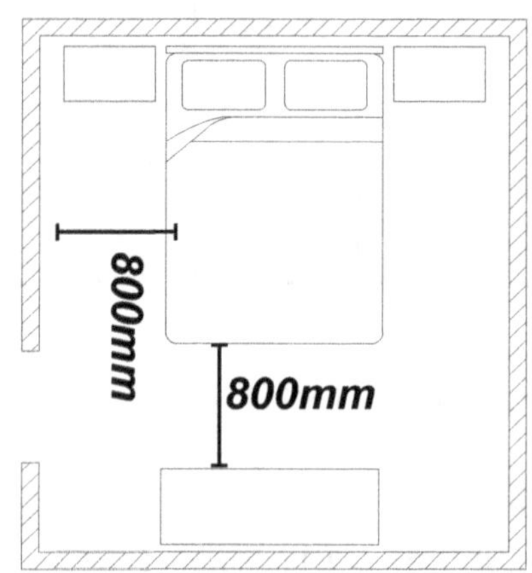


### *Twin Beds in a single room*
Minimum 800mm between beds is recommended, allowing for a shared nightstand and enough room for getting in and out of bed.

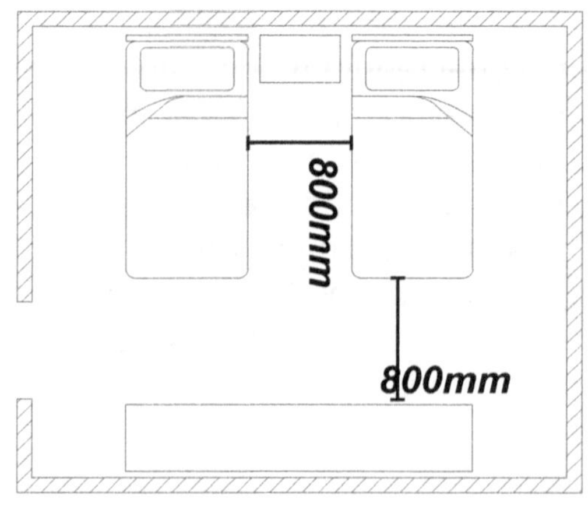

# BATHROOMS

Options for bathroom configurations range from small two-piece powder rooms to larger five-piece master bathroom suites. The examples on this page consist of an average size for bathrooms based totally on the range and proximity of furniture. For all bathroom layouts, comfort and privacy are the top priorities when designing a plan.

*Bathroom Layouts*

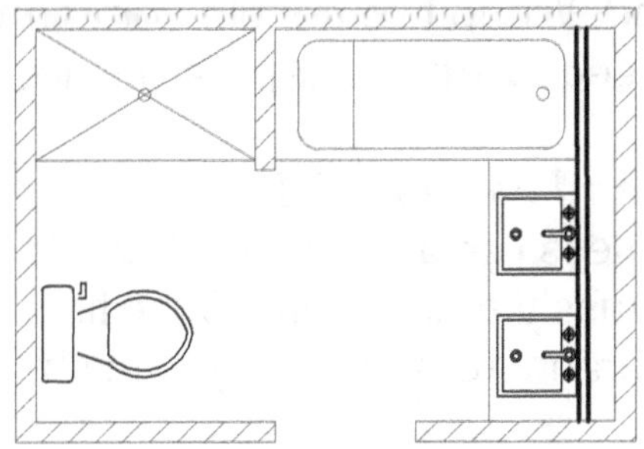

Four-Piece Bathroom
2590mm x 2130mm

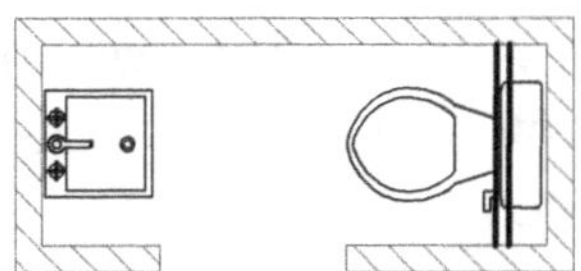

*Powder Room*
760mm x 1900mm

*Powder Room 2*
1370mm x 1220mm

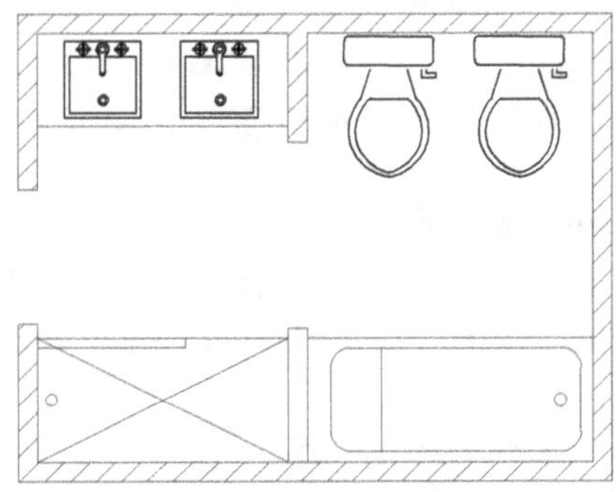

Five-Piece Bathroom
3500mm x 2590mm

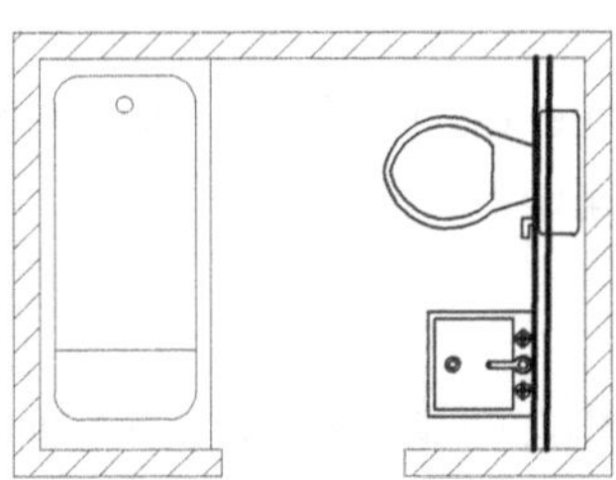

Typical Bathroom
2130mm x 1550mm

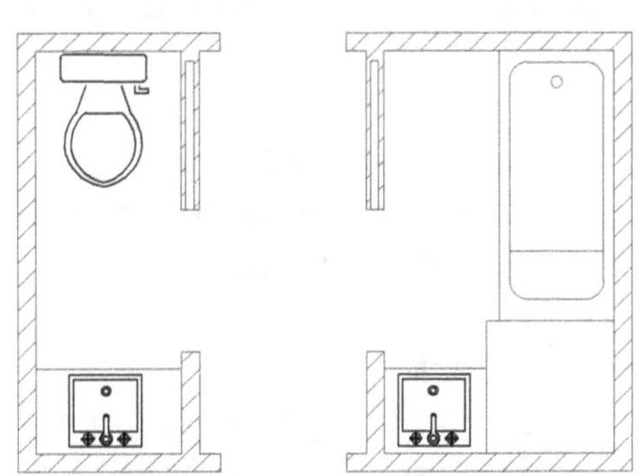

Two-Person Bathroom
3500mm x 1830mm

# THINGS TO REMEMBER

### Two-Person Use
Placing a bath and toilet in a single space is not ideal when the bathroom is shared. When two people commonly use a bathroom suite at the same time, an enclosed toilet or a separate toilet room should be considered if space allows.

### Wall and Floor Finishes
Countless options are available for floor and wall finishes for a bathroom, ceramic tile, glass tile and stone. Wall finishes need to be water-resistant with a waterproof membrane 1830mm above finish floor level, and floors need to be slip-resistant.

### Lighting
Bathrooms should include both general lighting and task lighting by the mirror and over the shower. The best mirror lighting is on the sides via wall sconces, which prevents no shadows on the face. Wall sconces should be placed approximately 1700mm above floor level and a minimum 760mm apart. Avoid using ceiling fixtures as the sole source of light. If the bathroom is small and there is not enough room for sidelights, consider introducing a light cove.

### Shower Controls
The many recent advances in shower design can make the selection of shower controls confusing. Here basic elements are defined:

### Spray Shower-head
A traditional shower-head that can be used in a shower enclosure or as part of a bath-shower combination mounted to the wall. It also comes in a variety of spray settings.

### High-flow Valve
Valves that control custom-designed showers with multiple spray heads, various manufacturers offer many features that are unique to their systems.

### Thermostatic-controlled Valve
A valve that allows the water temperature to be set while controlling the amount of water coming through the system at a precise temperature.

### Shower Diverter
Valve that redirects water from a spout to a shower-head or handheld shower. A two-way diverter is for a bathtub and shower combination. These diverters can be as simple as a pull-tab on the tub spout that redirects the water flow from one function to the other.

CHAPTER EIGHT

# RESTAURANT ENVIRONMENTS

# RESTAURANT ENVIRONMENTS

Restaurant types vary from fast-food to completely serviced restaurants with distinct styles and dining zones. Restaurant design includes a great number of problems concerning adjacencies, kitchen designs, lighting fixtures, acoustics, and so forth. The interior designer should be familiar with each scenario, specifically with the dimensional criteria for seating layouts.

Before outlining the seating layout, the interior designer should understand the restaurant concept. The concept should outline the form of dining experience offered, the intended clientele, the hours of operation, and the menu. If the client's idea is to place the chef within the kitchen on display, for example, then the seating needs to be arranged so that the kitchen is visible from each table. Furthermore, the spacing among tables will have a substantial effect on the person dining at the restaurant. Tables closely packed together will result in a loud and active space, because people need to compete with their friends to be heard. Conversely, tables spaced further apart tend to split diners into quieter pockets of conversation.

### Types of Seating:

Restaurant seating falls into three distinct zones: Built-in seating comprising of banquettes and booths, Lose seating and bar seating. Seat-pad heights are typically 435mm to 465mm for a dining table and low counter-tops. Bar seating typically ranges from 760mm to 865mm. Any seats within a dining environment should be a minimum of 400mm. For a completely serviced dining experience, consider the use of padded seating and upholstered armchairs for getting in and out of the seat, which will also add an additional level of luxury.

### Tables and Counters:

Within a restaurant setting, tables are referred to as tops. The most common sizes are two tops (seating two people) and four tops (seating four people). Beyond those sizes, tables are normally mixed or expanded. Some tables have flip-up corners, which convert a square top seating four to a round table seating six. Table heights are generally 720mm. A round table with a size of 900mm across can accommodate four people. A square table with a measurement of 600mm across is suitable for 2; but, 750 mm is most beneficial. Smaller tables are applicable when only drink service is supplied. Counters range in height from 700mm to 900mm; but, In America with Disabilities Act (ADA) calls for 1500mm of the counter be no more than 865mm high to accommodate customers in wheelchairs.

# MINIMUM TABLE DIMENSIONS

| Shape | Seats | Width (W) | Length (L) |
|---|---|---|---|
| Square | 2 | 610mm x 760mm | 610mm - 760mm |
| Square | 4 | 900mm | 900mm |
| Round | 4 | 900mm - 1100mm | |
| Round | 6 | 1050mm - 1250mm | |
| Round | 8 - 10' | 1650mm | |
| Rectangulur | 4 (2per side) | 800mm - 800mm | 1050mm x 1200mm |
| Rectangulur | 6 (3per side) | 750mm - 900mm | 1800mm x 2100mm |
| Rectangulur | 8 (2per side) | 900mm | 2300mm x 2700mm |

## Tables showing minimum table sizes

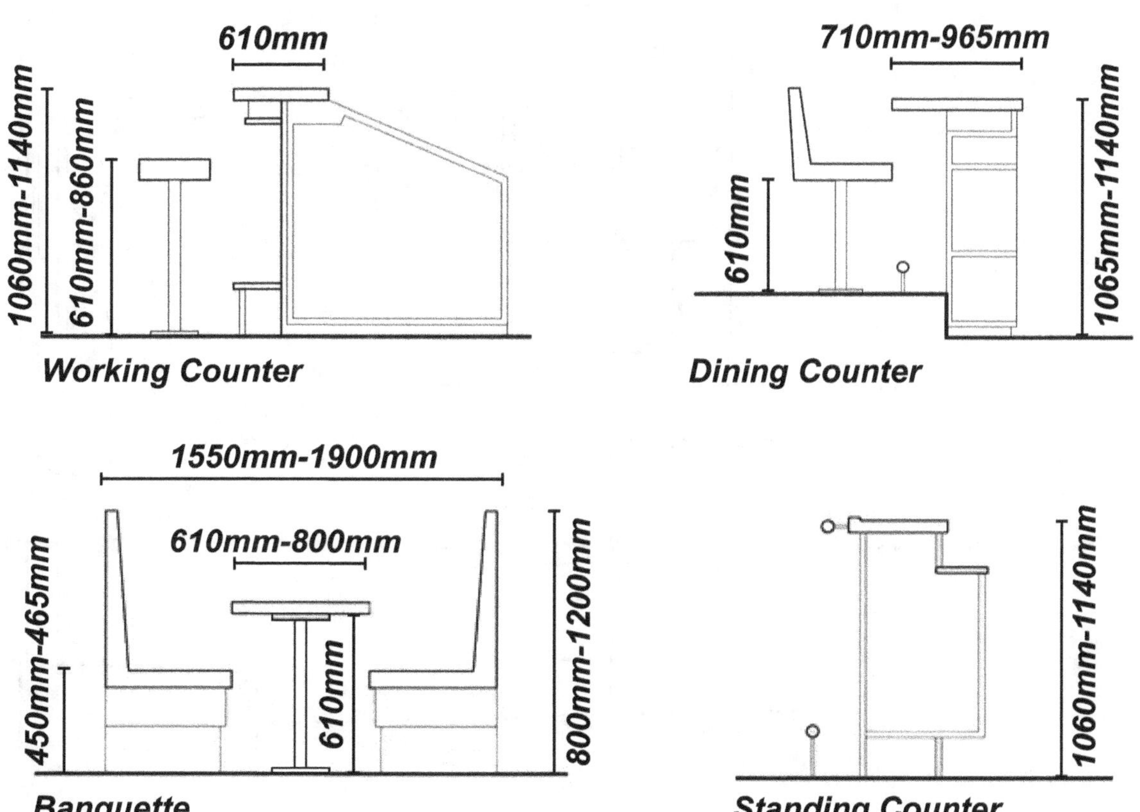


These sections describe ideal vertical dimensions. Please note that all vertical dimensions are subject to local building code and accessibility regulations.

# TYPICAL RESTAURANT LAYOUT

*A Banquette*

*B Table Setting*

*C Bar Seating*

*D Wall Seating*

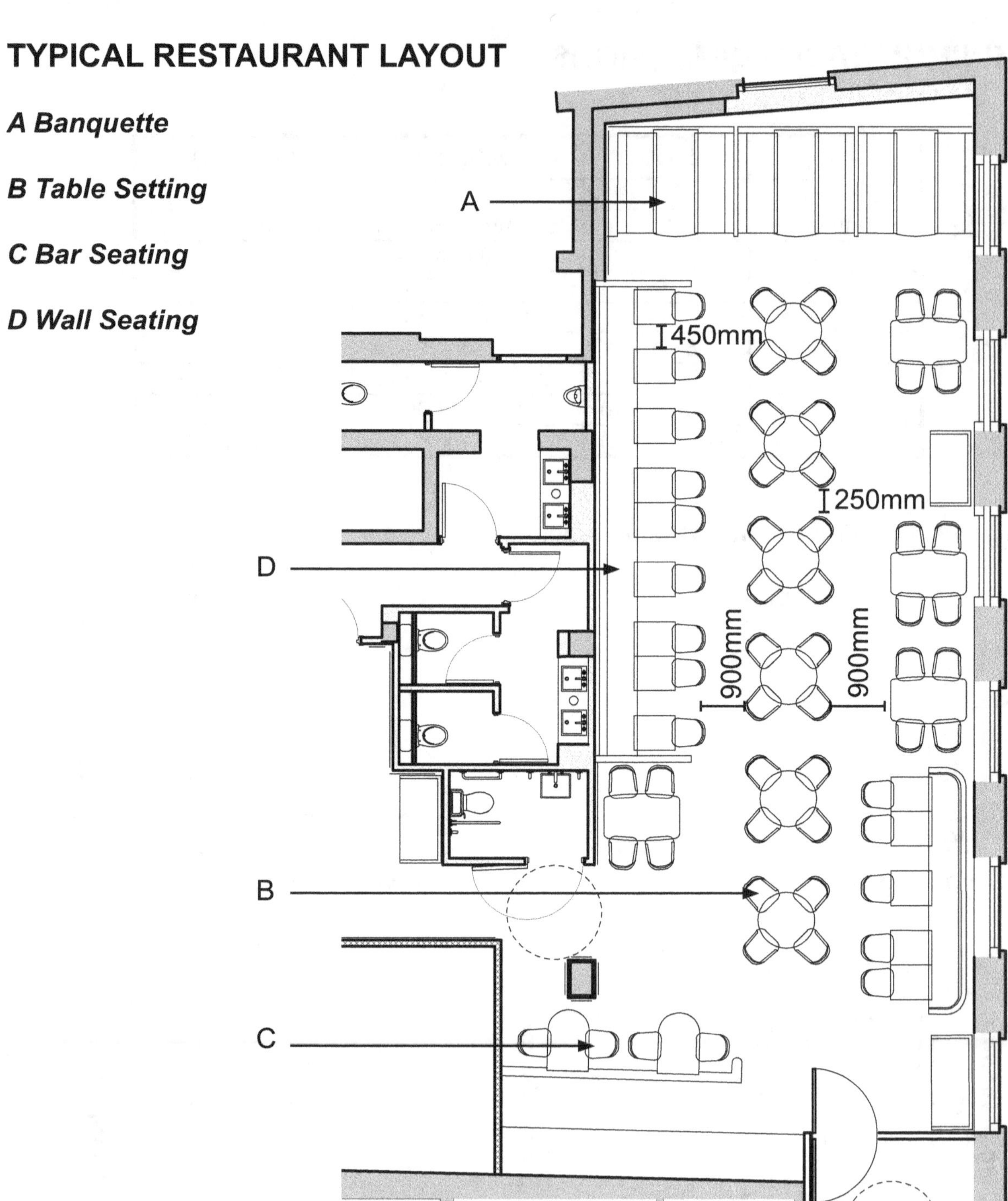


The plan notes minimal dimensions for access routes, limited passage, and no passage routes. Wheelchair accessible aisles are required from the restaurant's entrance to the accessible seating and restrooms.

# THINGS TO REMEMBER

## *Spacing between Tables*
As long as the spacing among tables meets the minimum dimensions required
for an access route, the spacing is driven generally by the restaurant. Fully
serviced restaurants provide greater space between furniture for a relaxed dining
experience, while fast-food restaurants maximise the number of seats. The access
route size is decided through the local building code, which specifies a minimum
width of 900mm for the access route and also calls for that all accessible tables be
located adjacent to an access route.

## *Interior Finishes*
Interior finishes and textures are the most tangible elements that an interior
designer can use to explain and express the quality of a restaurant. In reality,
materials suitable for the general public areas will vary from the ones appropriate
for a kitchen; however, in each area, fire-retardant materials need to be utilised.
Further to the quality of the materials specified, it is essential to consider their
maintenance properties to make sure their suitability for the type of restaurant, and
the amount of traffic that a specific area will see.

## *Lighting*
The lighting design will determine the ambience of a restaurant. Low-level mood
lighting is typically used for fine dining, while bright lighting offers a casual dining
experience. Over the course of a day, a restaurant can change the lighting levels
to suggest different moods. Most restaurant lighting is incandescent (warm-white
2700Kv) because of the warm tones that the lamps provide; however, fluorescent
lighting is more energy-efficient and may be more appropriate in the kitchen areas.

## *Acoustics*
The acoustics in a restaurant goes hand-in-hand with the concept. In many
restaurants, for example, the reverberation of hard surfaces adds to the desired
effect of the dining experience. There are many ways to control the acoustics in
an environment, as long as the desired result is understood. The easiest way
to control acoustics is through sound-absorbent materials. They can range from
carpet on the floor to fabric panelling on the walls to fabric applied to the underside
of the tables, to sound absorptive tiles in the ceiling. Another strategy worth
considering is to partition the restaurant into different types of rooms with varying
levels of noise to suit the various clientele.

# #3 Finer Details

The components of an interior design fall into
two categories:

**Fixed elements**
such as walls, mouldings, light fixtures, and
built-in cabinetry.

**Movable elements**
such as furniture, artwork, and the curiosities
and ephemera that are evidence of everyday
life.

Significantly, the selection of movable objects
requires a close collaboration between the
interior designer and client. Smaller items
play an extremely large role in suggesting the
interests and tastes of their owners. Artwork
and souvenirs can also have very personal
associations. As a result, interior designers often
serve as teachers, by investigating both the
taste of their clients and the objects they own
into a larger vision for an interior. A good interior
designer will empower clients to make their own
smart curatorial decisions long after the project
is finished.

# 09

## CHAPTER NINE

# DETAILS

Key to the successful mixture of materials, colours, textures, and patterns is how the elements of an interior are specified. While detailing will range from project to project, there are standard details with which each designer must be familiar.

## *Fire-Rated Wall Assemblies*

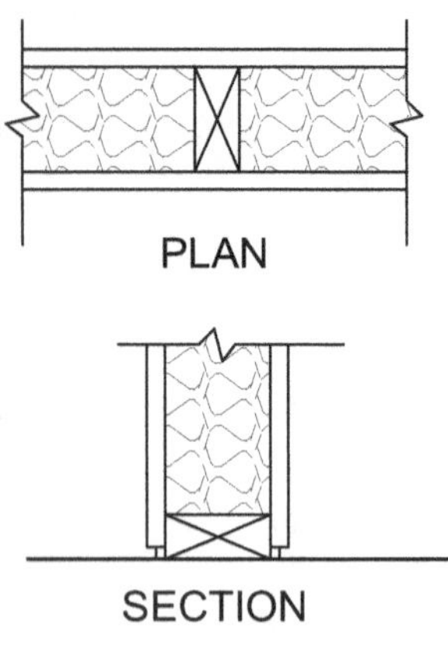


### *1-Hour-Rated Assemble*
1 layer 16mm gypsum wallboard on each side of 38mm × 99mm studs at 400mm centres. Acoustic sealant top and bottom.

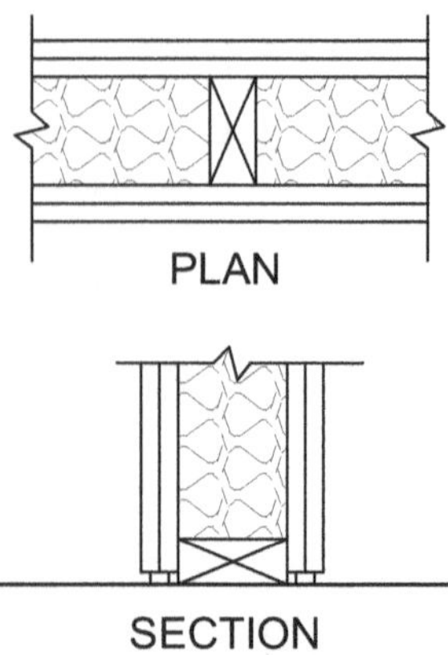


### *2-Hour-Rated Assembly*
2 layers 16mm gypsum wallboard on each side of 38mm × 99mm studs at 400mm centres. Acoustic sealant top and bottom.

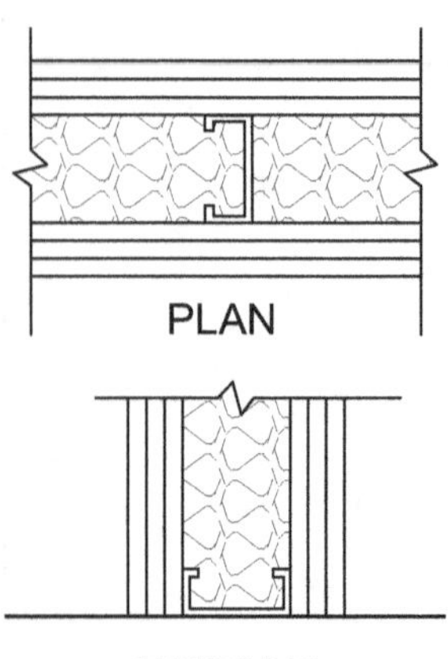


### *2-Hour-Rated Assembly*
3 layers 16mm gypsum wallboard on each side of 38mm × 99mm studs at 400mm centres. Acoustic sealant top and bottom.

## *Sound Proofing Wall Assemblies*

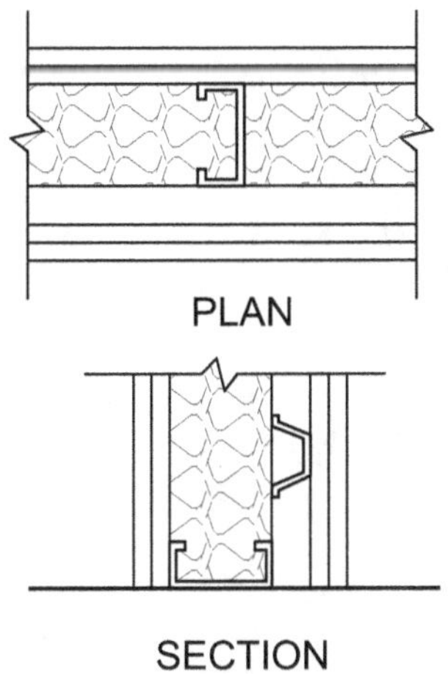



### *STC 40–47*
2 layers 16mm each side of 38mm × 99mm studs at 400mm centres. Furring channel one side. Acoustic sealant top and bottom.

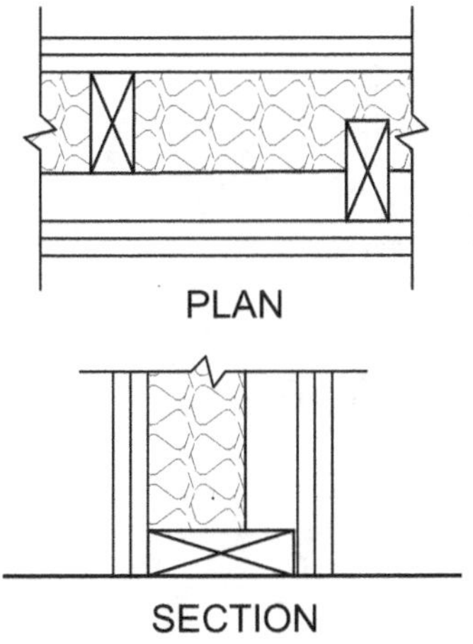



### *STC 50–54*
2 layers 16mm each side of 38mm × 99mm studs at 400mm centres. Studs staggered to create an air pocket—acoustic sealant top and bottom.

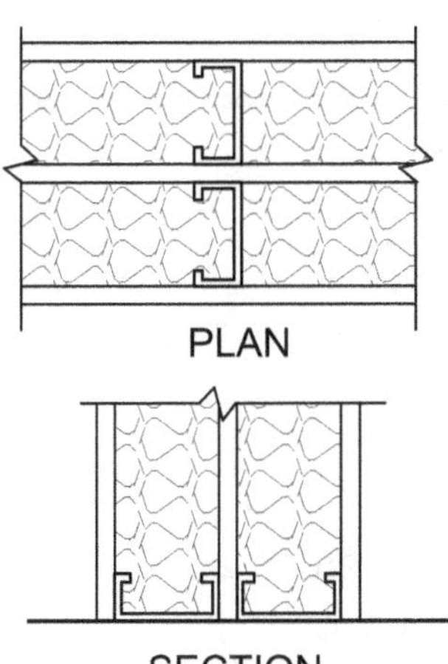



### *STC 56-61*
1 layer 16mm gypsum wallboard on each side of 38mm × 99mm studs at 400mm centres. Studs nominally separated—acoustic sealant top and bottom.

# PARTITIONS ON EXISTING WALLS

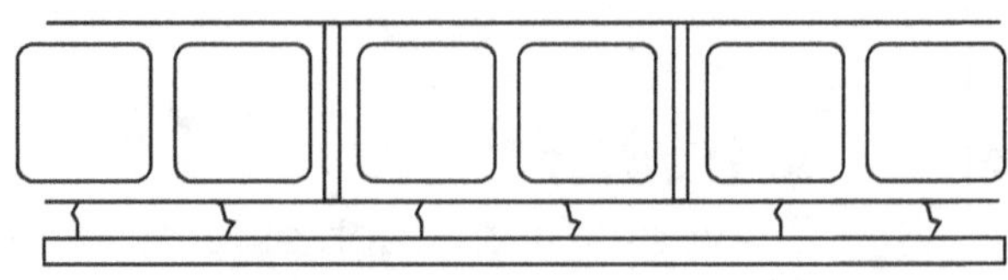

PLAN

### *Dot and Dab*
Dabs of adhesive every 200mm to 300mm); to the back of the (GWB).

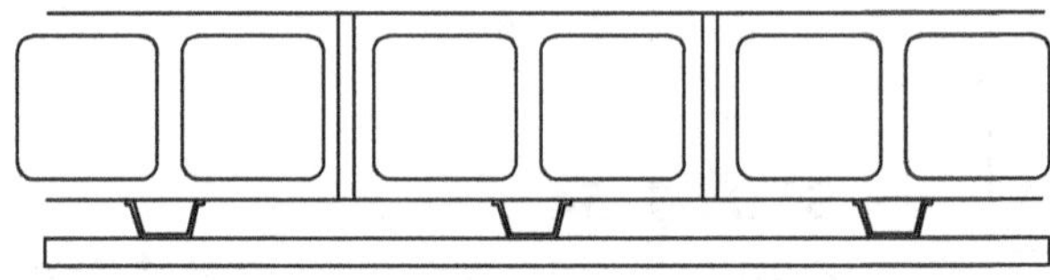

PLAN

### *Direct to Structure*
Furring channel at 400mm. 1 layer 16mm GWB.

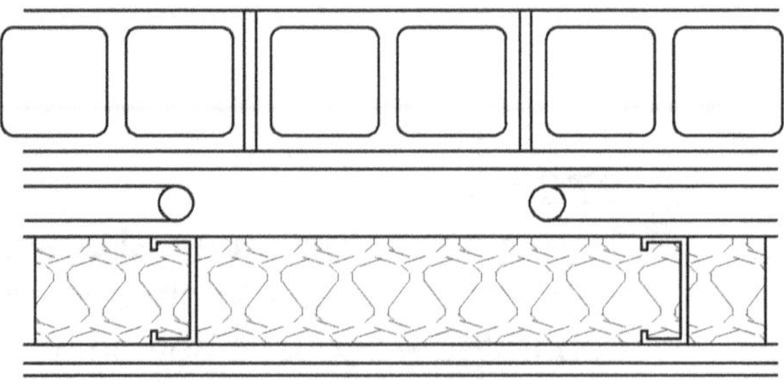

PLAN

### *Structure with Mechanical*
1 layer 16mm GWB one side of 38mm × 99mm studs at 400mm centres. Tie back to wall with metal clips.

## Base Profiles

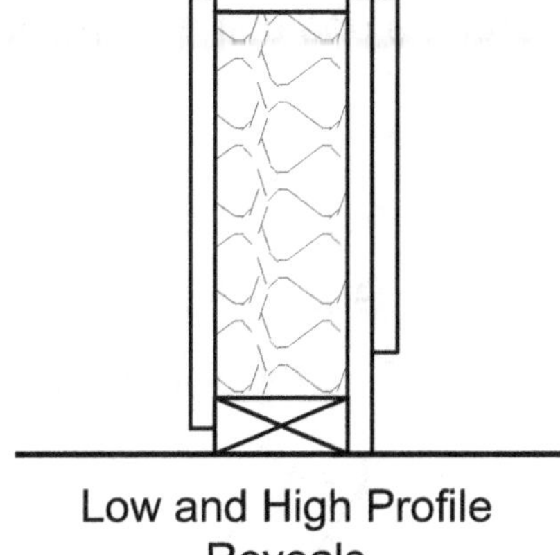

Low and High Profile
Reveals

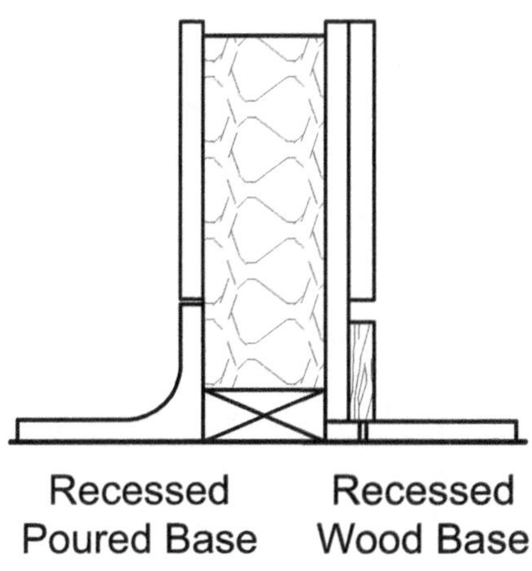

Recessed      Recessed
Poured Base   Wood Base

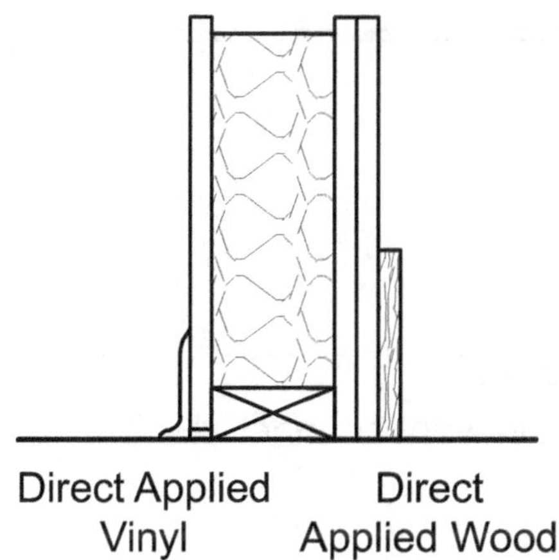

Direct Applied    Direct
Vinyl    Applied Wood

## Corner Profiles

Inside Corner with
Reveal One Side

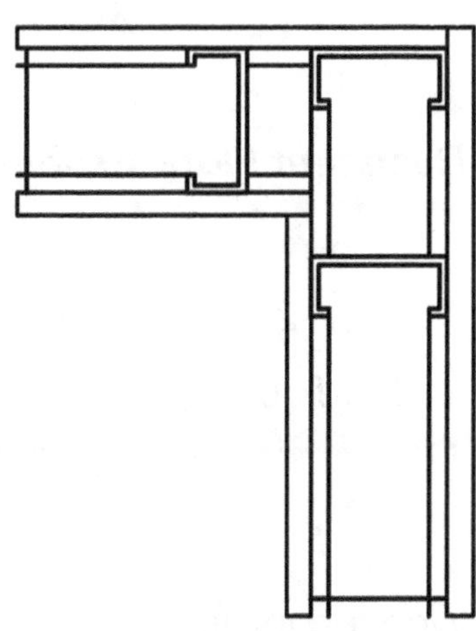

Typical Outside Corner

# FLOORING CONSTRUCTION

### *Slab-On-Grade Foundation*

Slab-on-grade foundation with floor and footing poured as one unit and the floor at, or only slightly above, ground level.

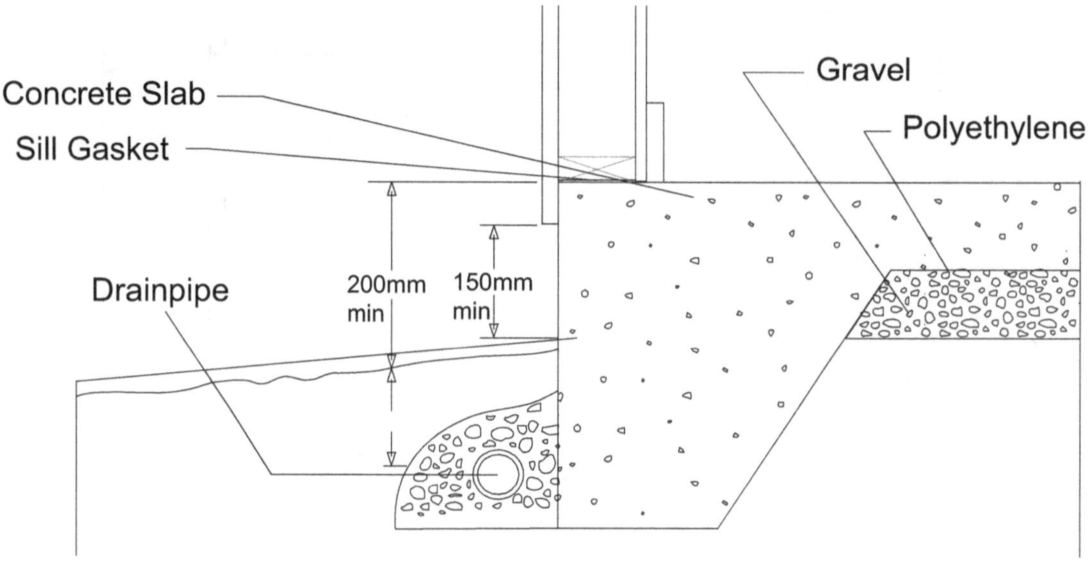



### *Noise-Resistant Floor Assembly*

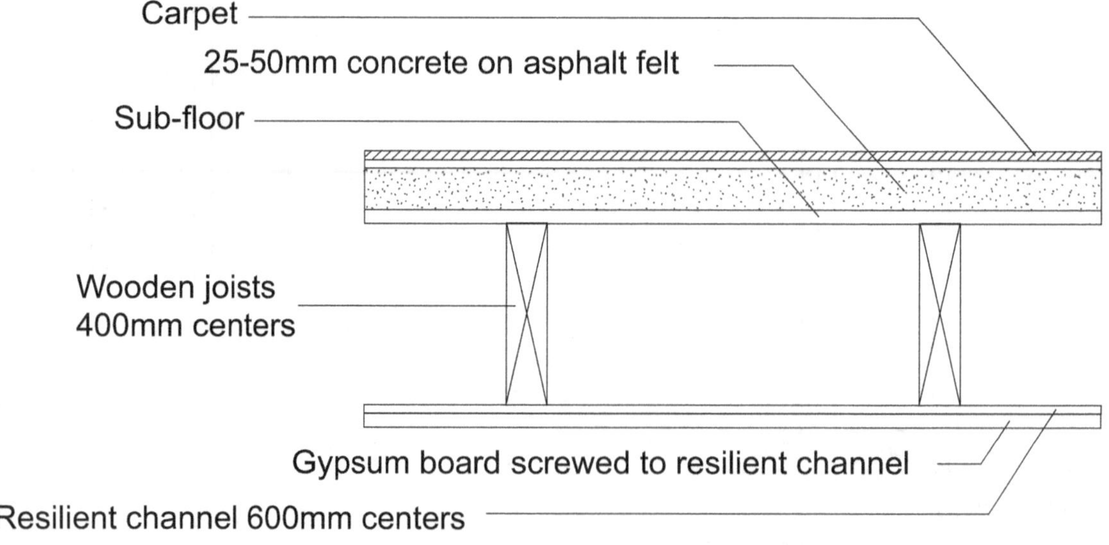

## *Concrete Masonry Crawl Space Foundation*

Crawl space foundation with unfinished dirt floor at or below adjacent ground level.

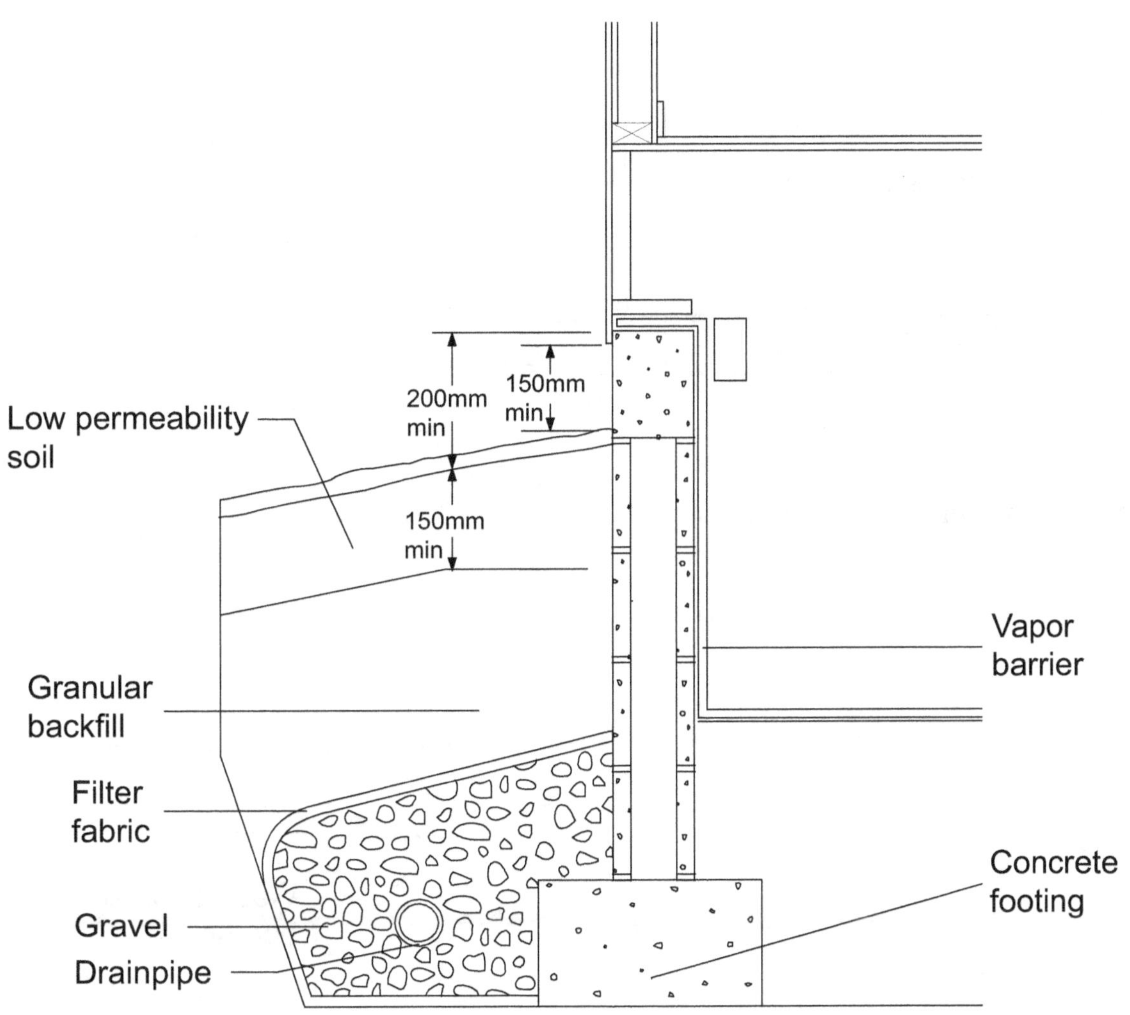

# EXTERNAL DOOR SILL CONSTRUCTION

Sill flashing installation to sliding glass door opening.

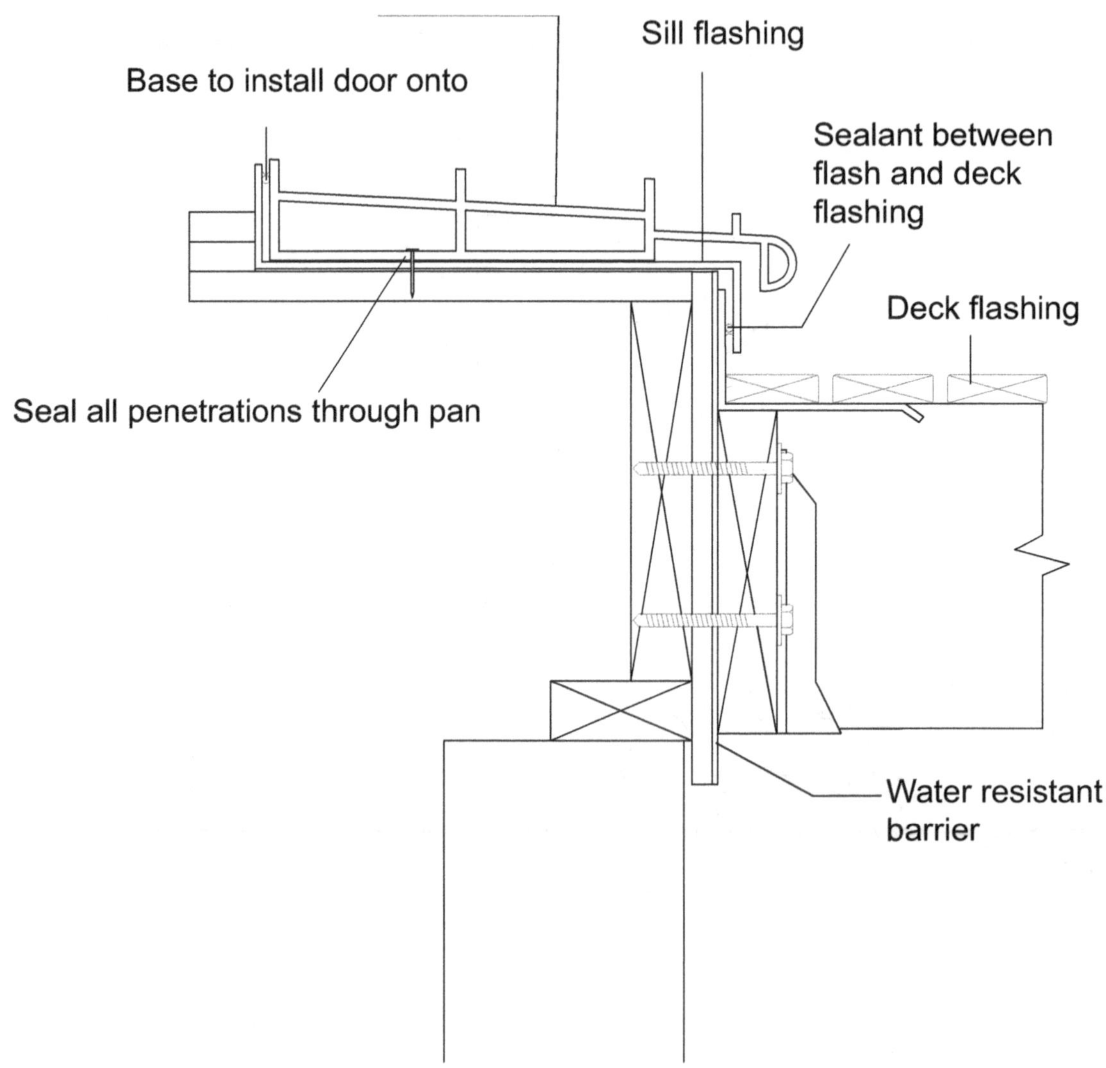

# EXTERNAL WINDOW CONSTRUCTION

Cross-section of window opening showing integration of structure's water-resistive system in a wall with brick veneer.

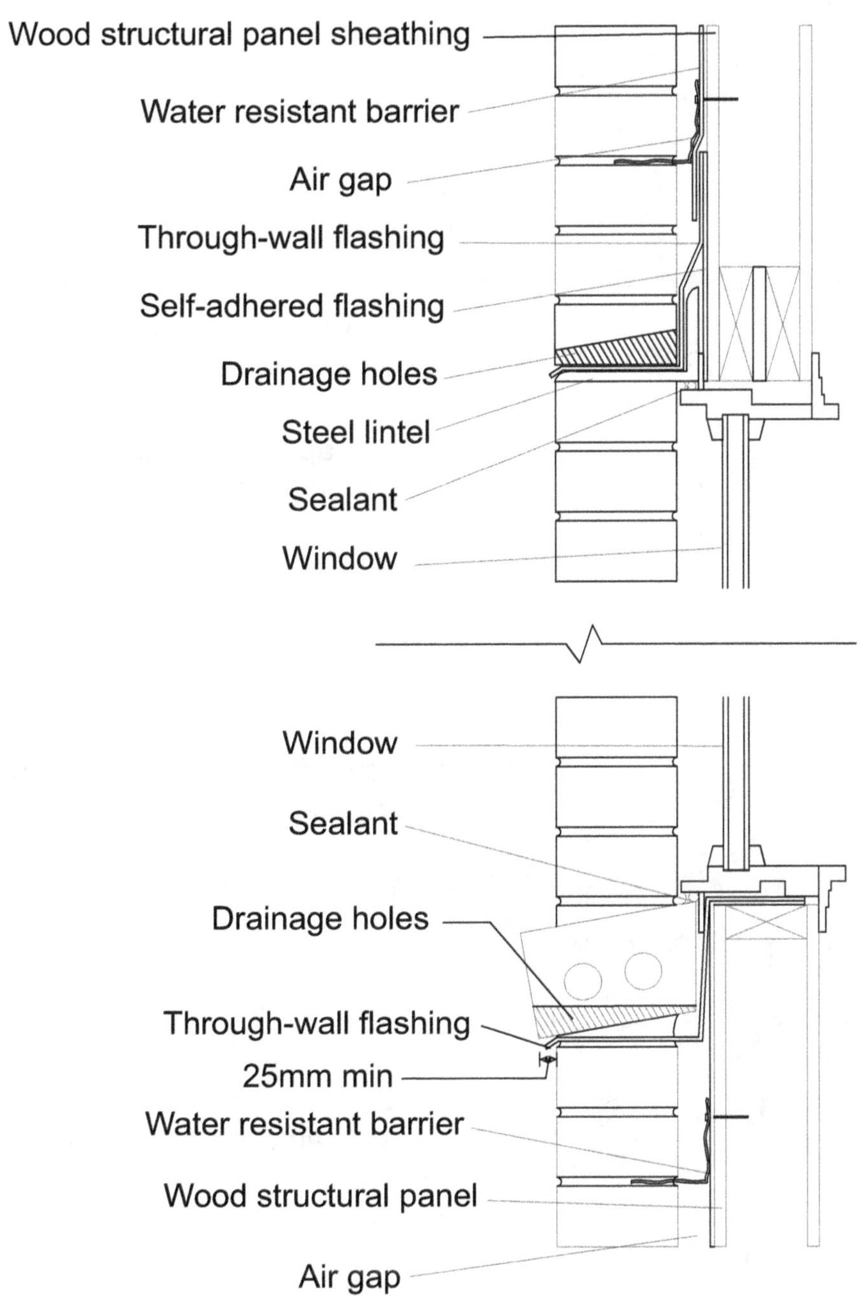

# ROOFING CONSTRUCTION

## *Closed Soffit*

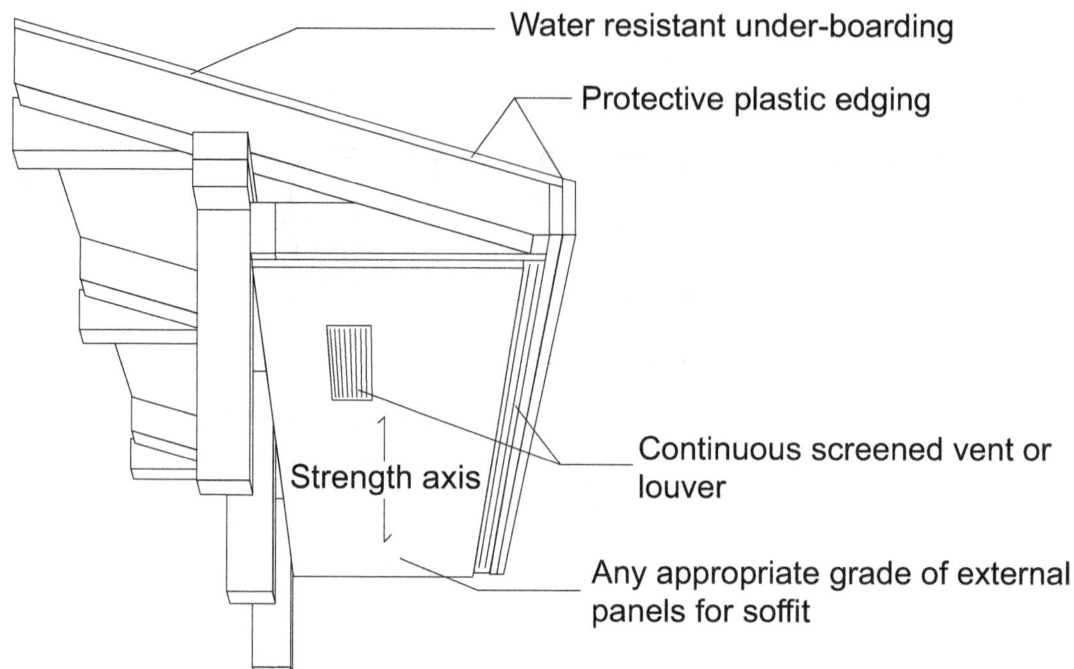


## *Open Soffit*

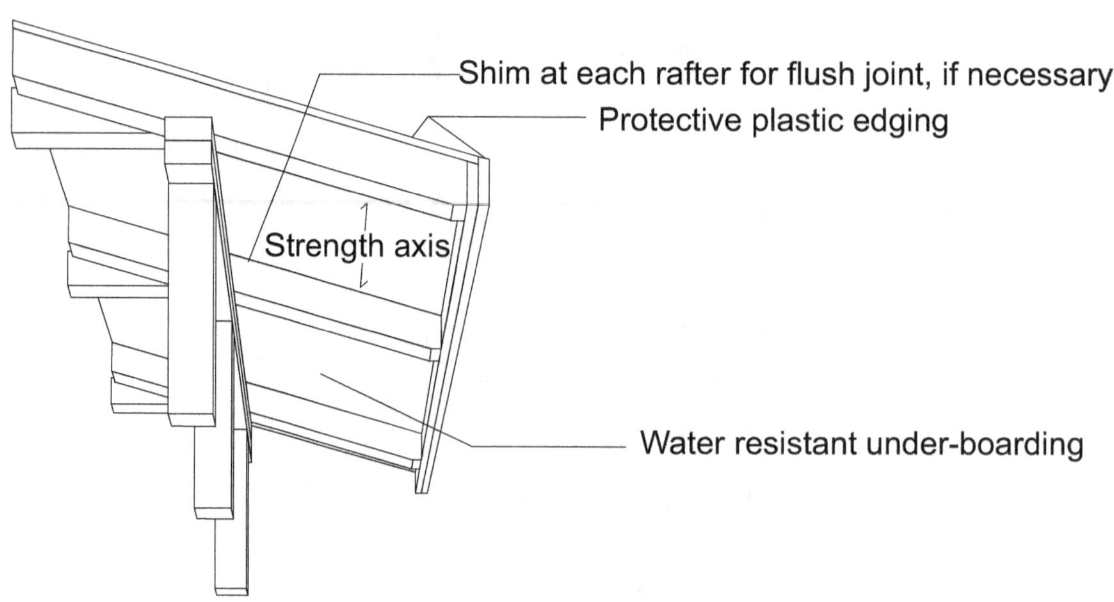

# ROOF CONSTRUCTION STYLES

Choosing the right design for a roof is very important. Although rather underestimated, roofs play a vital role within the safety and overall structural capacity of the building, which means deciding on the correct roof. Needs to be done correctly and with the utmost care and concern.

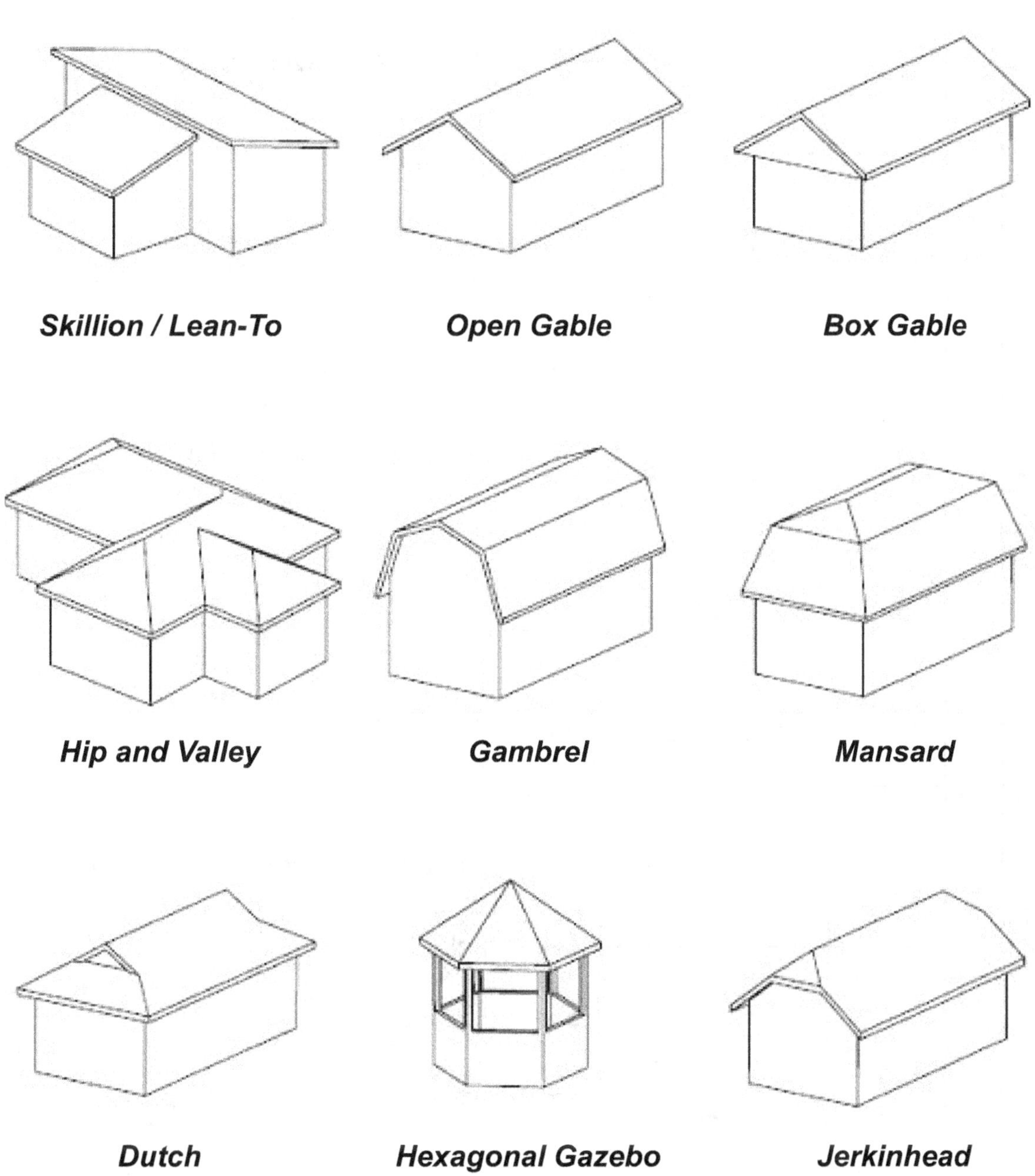

# CABINETS

## *Typical Base and Upper Cabinet*

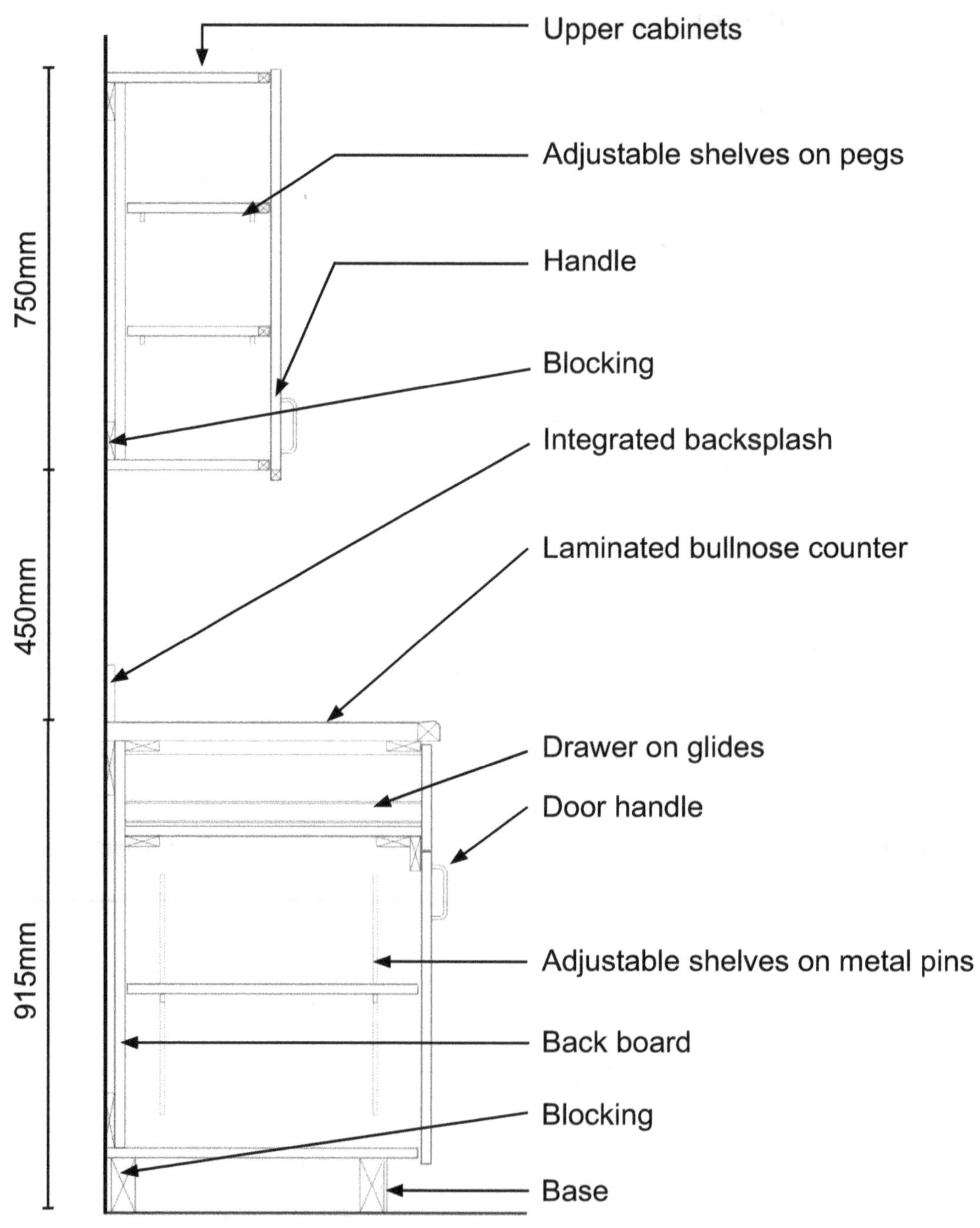

# TYPICAL COUNTER EDGES

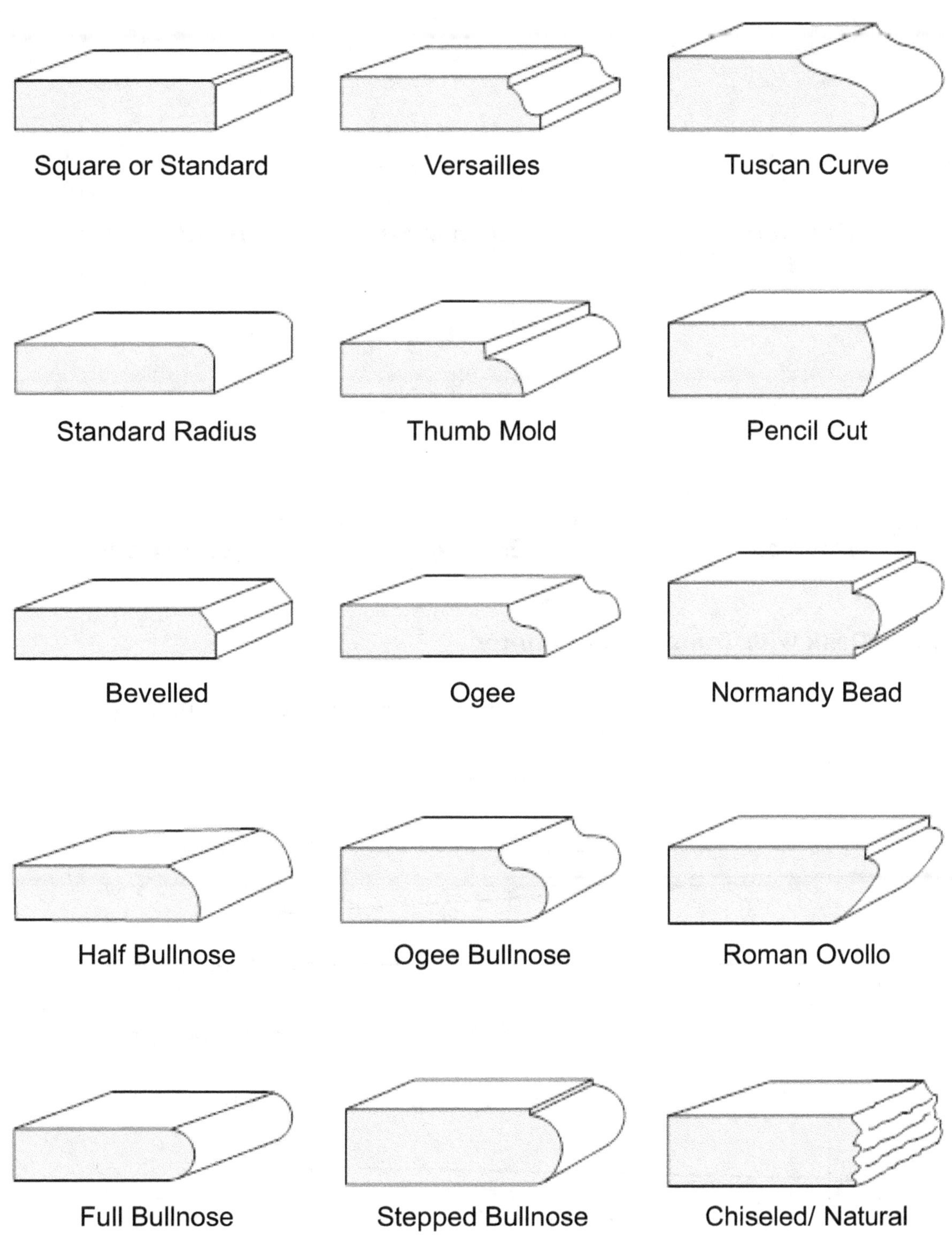

# JOINERY TYPES

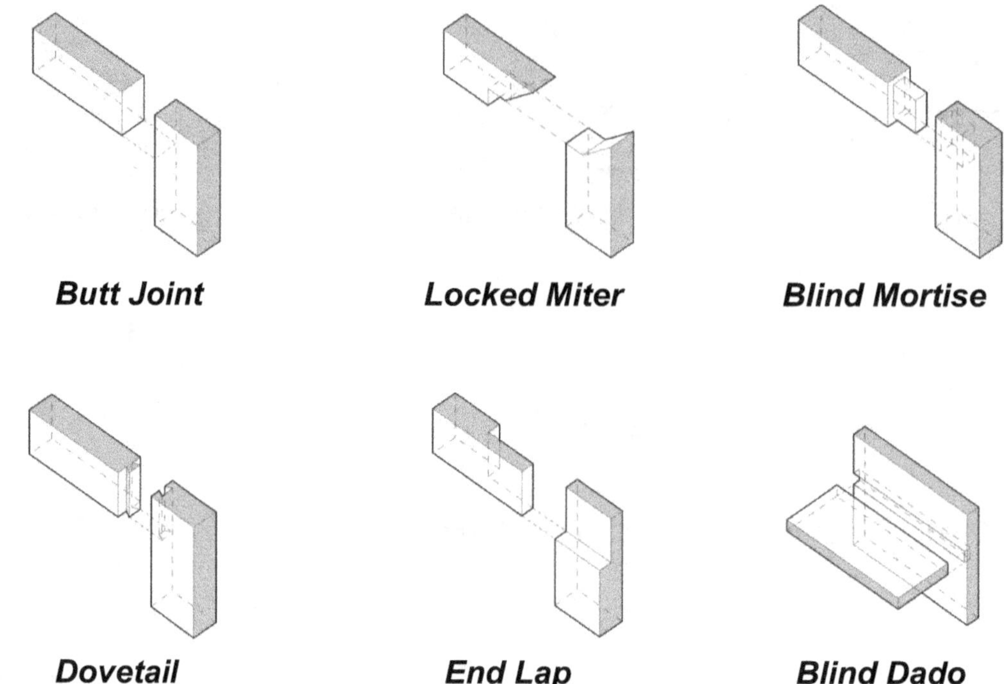



## *Typical Desk with Transaction Counter*

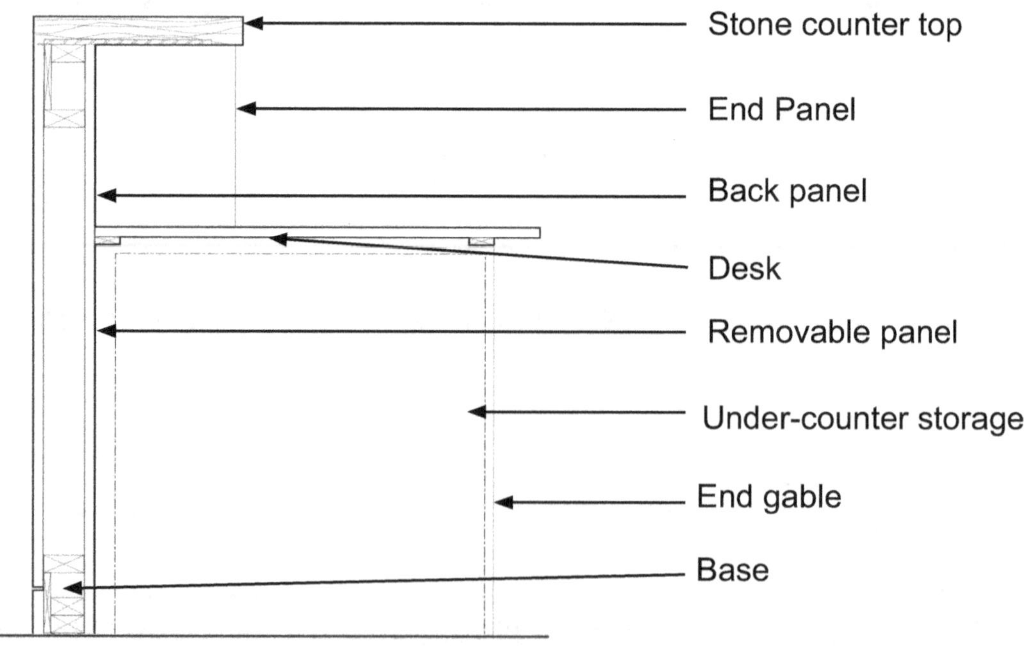

# CEILINGS

## *Ceiling Profiles*

1 - Hung ceiling with furring channel
2 - Stud attached directly to channel
3 - Acoustic membrane
4 - Corner tape

1 - wall assembly with steel stud soffit
2 - hung ceiling with furring channel
3 - control joint taped and sanded
4 - furring channel either side

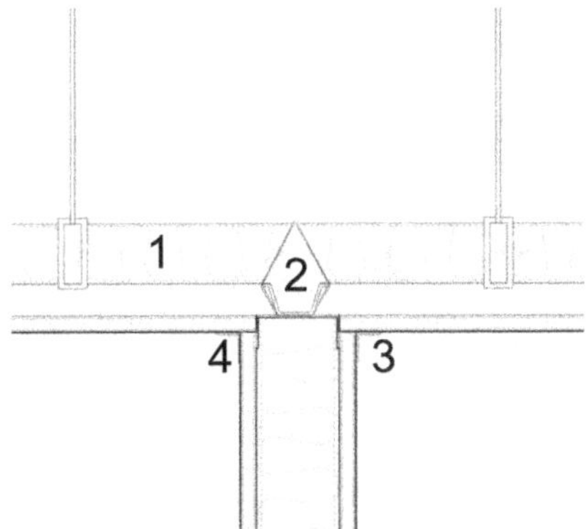

**Wall to Underside of Ceiling**

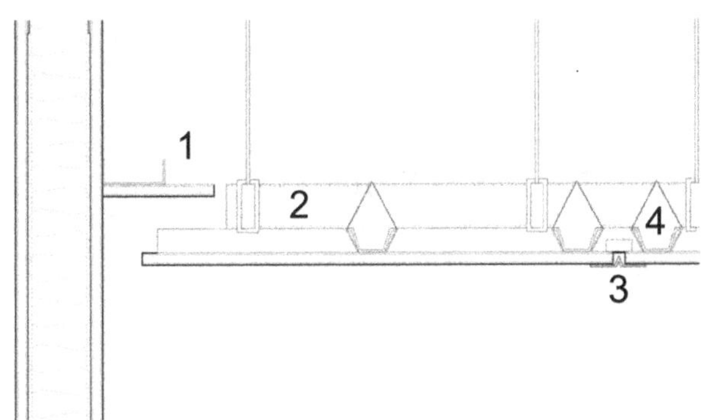

**Return-Air Slot  -  Control Joint**

1 - Hung ceiling with furring channel
2 - Shadow gap
3 - Steel stud framed corner

1 - Suspended ceiling assembly
2 - Shadow gap
3 - Return GWB to ceiling end

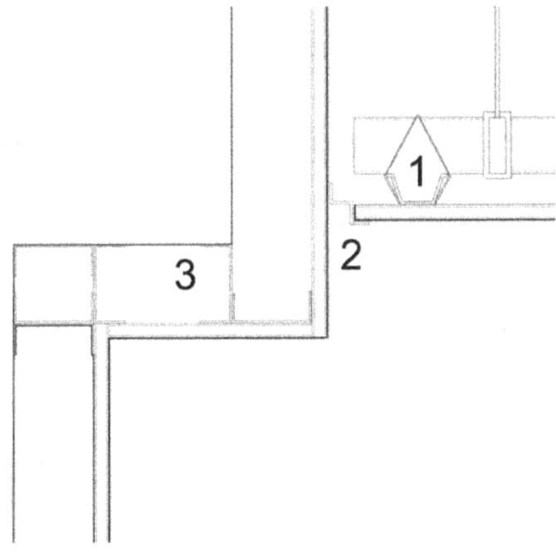

**GWB Soffit**

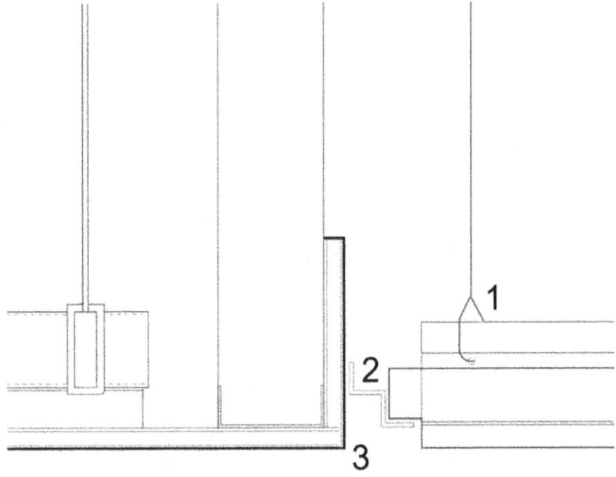

**GWB to Suspended Ceiling**

# CEILING LIGHTING

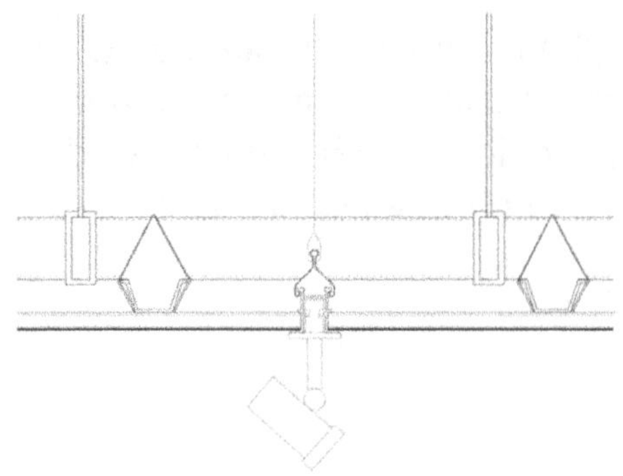

**Recessed Track Lighting**

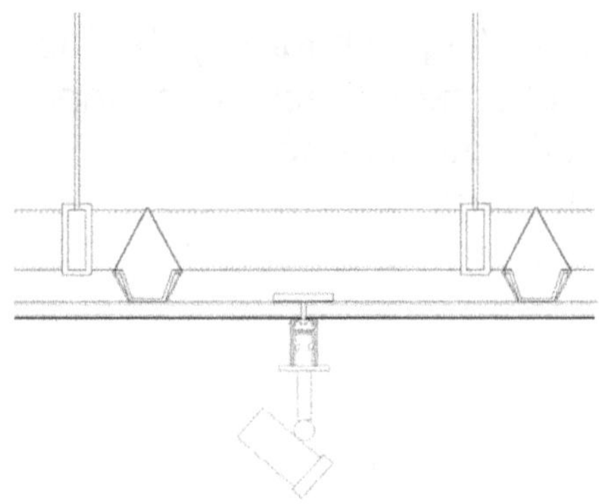

**Surface Track Lighting**

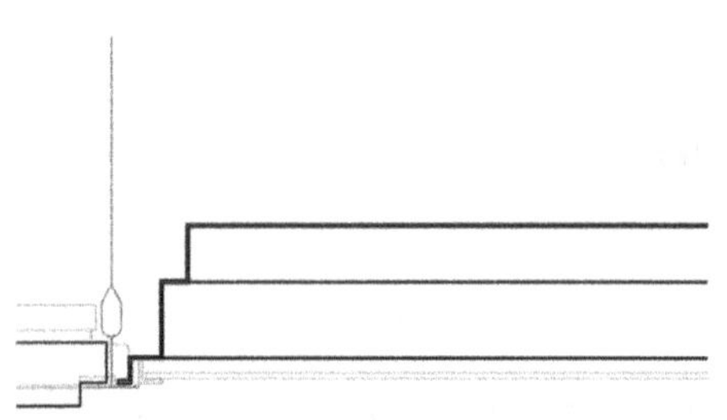

**Fluorescent Lighting**

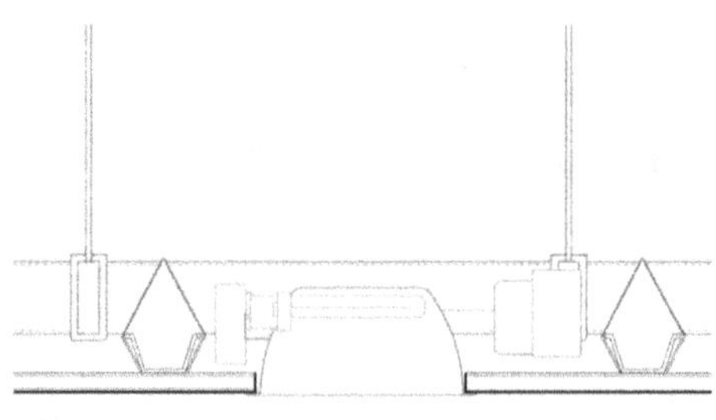

**Recessed Light Fixture**

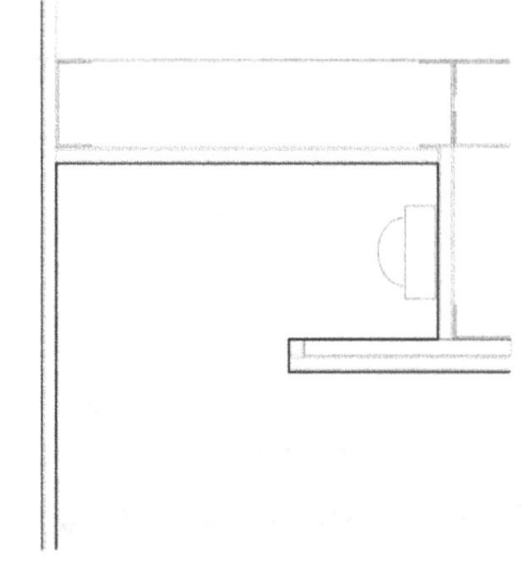

**Coffer Accent Lighting**

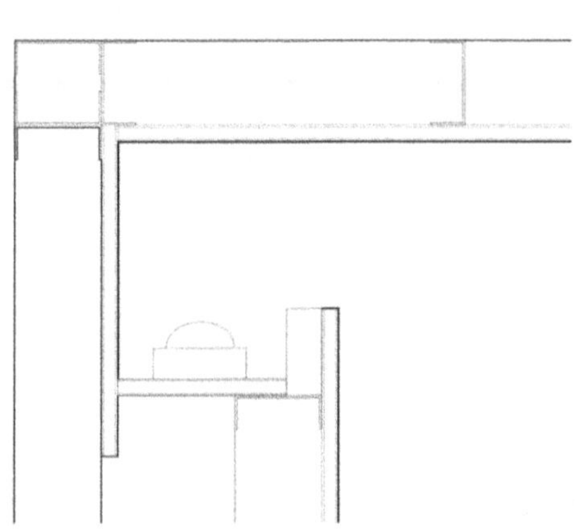

**Coffer Up lighting**

# TYPICAL BAR COUNTER-TOP DIMENSIONS

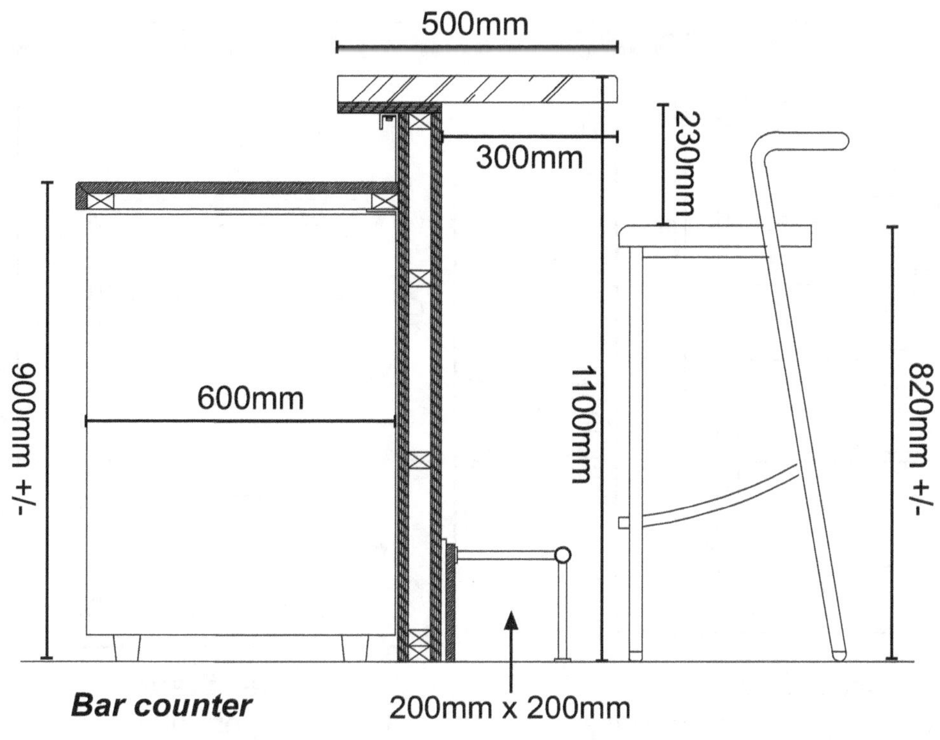



*Bar counter*

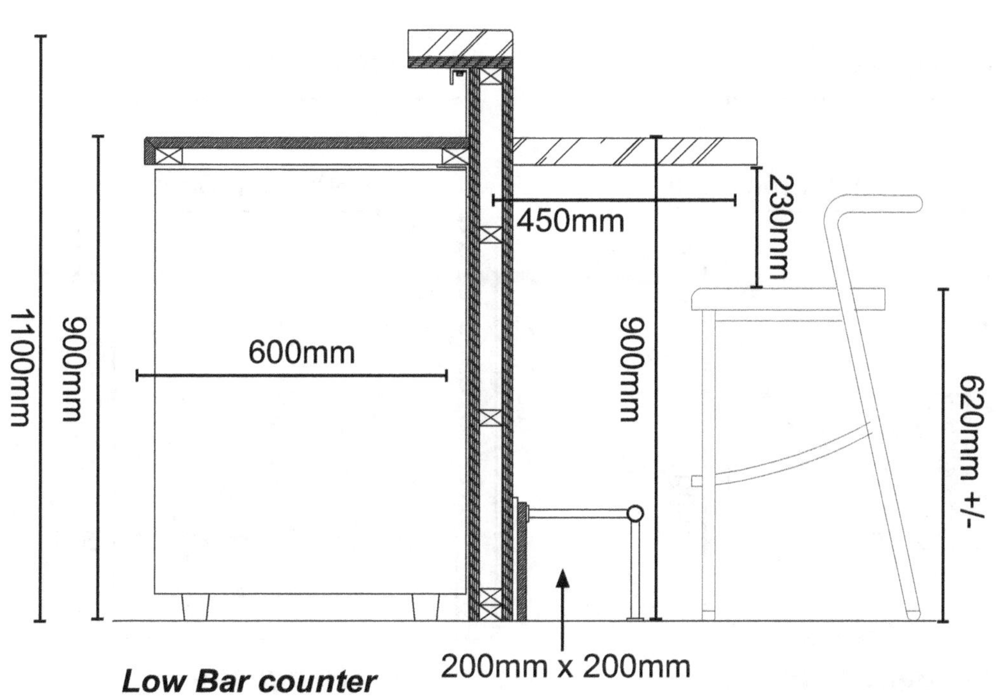



*Low Bar counter*

# TYPICAL RESTAURANT DIMENSIONS

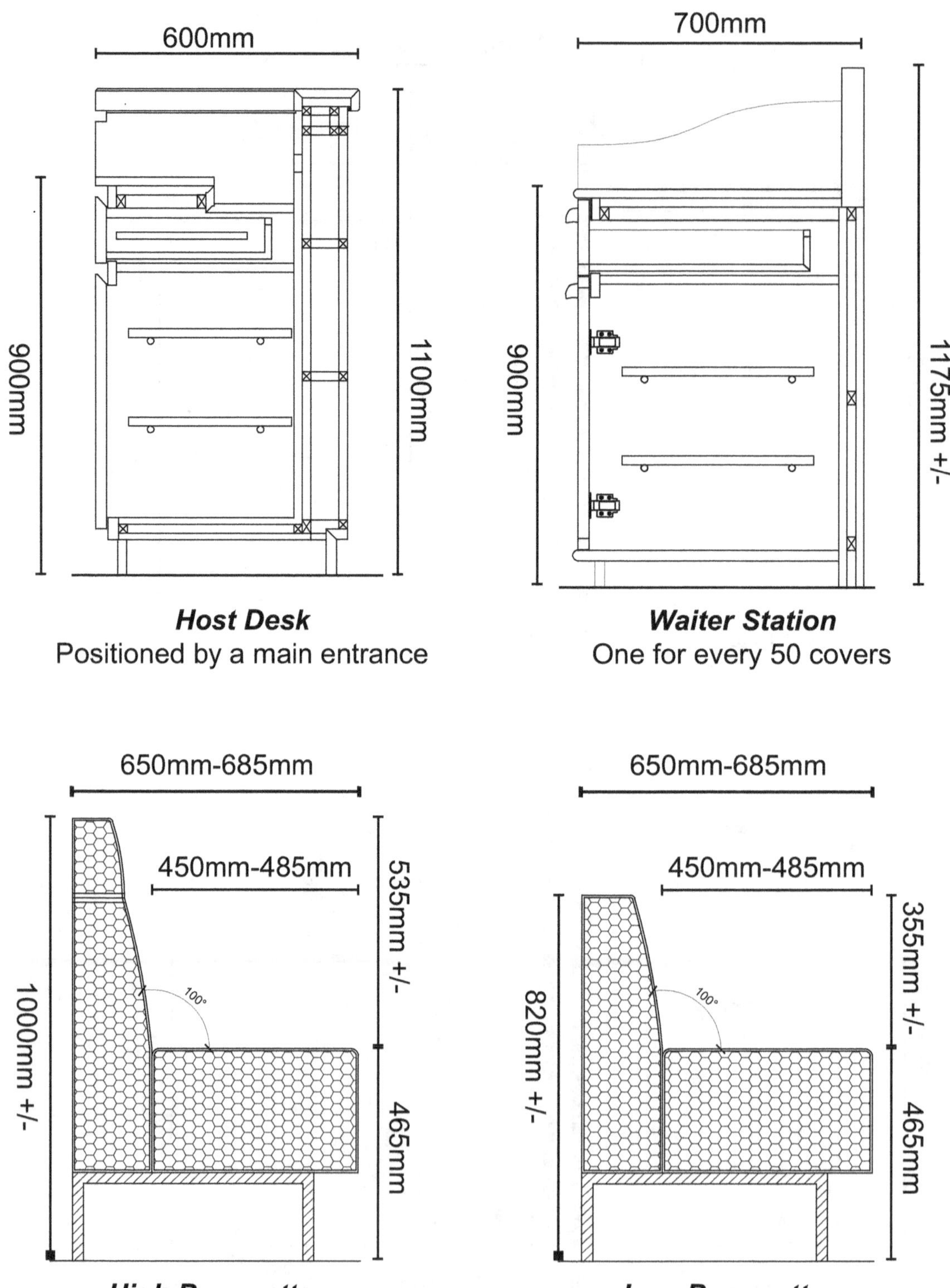



**Host Desk**
Positioned by a main entrance

**Waiter Station**
One for every 50 covers

**High Banquette**

**Low Banquette**

# DOORS AND HARDWARE

## Door Types

# BUTT HINGES

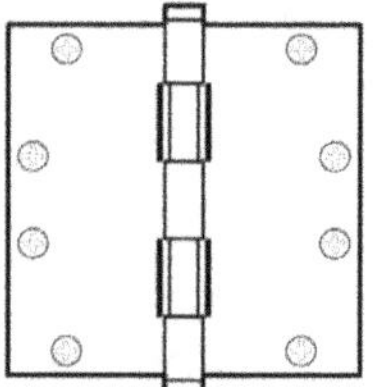

A plain bearing butt hinge is the most common hinge used to hang a door.

**Butt Hinge**

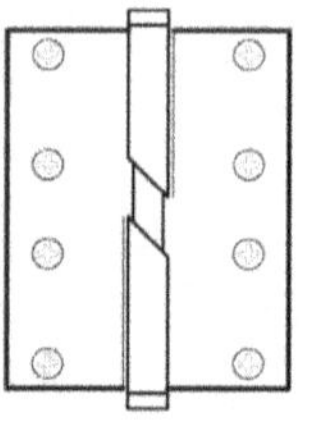

This hinge varying floor levels by allowing the door to lift.

**Self-Closing Hinge**

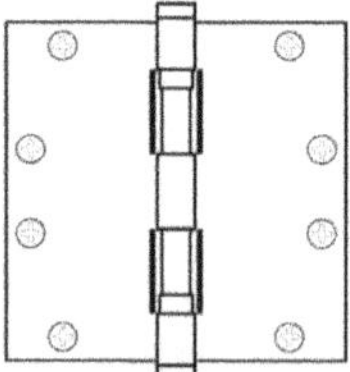

Should be specified for heavy doors, with closers, or doors in high traffic areas.

**Ball-Bearing Hinge**

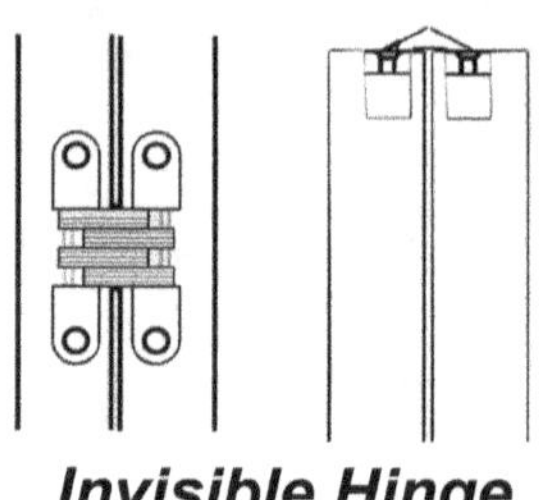

Invisible when the door is closed and can open 180 degrees.

**Invisible Hinge**

# PIVOT HINGE

## Offset Pivot Hinge

Hinge offsets the pivot away from the door and allows the door to swing 180 degrees.

## Center Pivot Hinge

Hinge is centred on the pivot point and, in the absence of a doorstop, allows the door to swing in two directions.

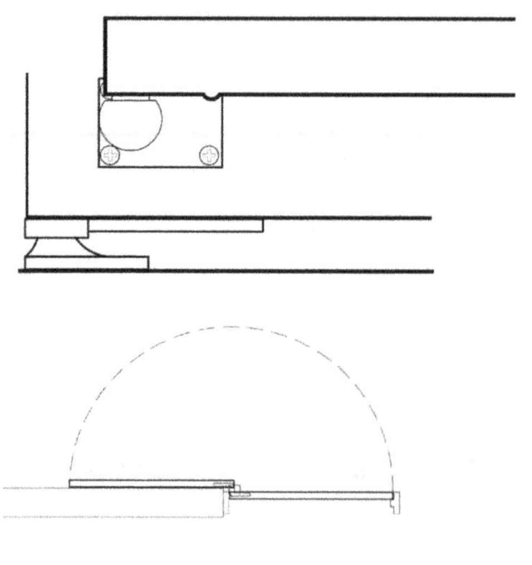

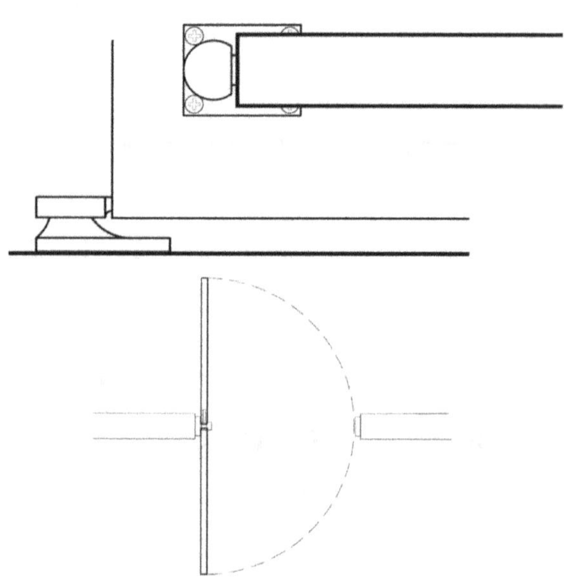

# FLOORING PATTERNS AND TRANSITIONS

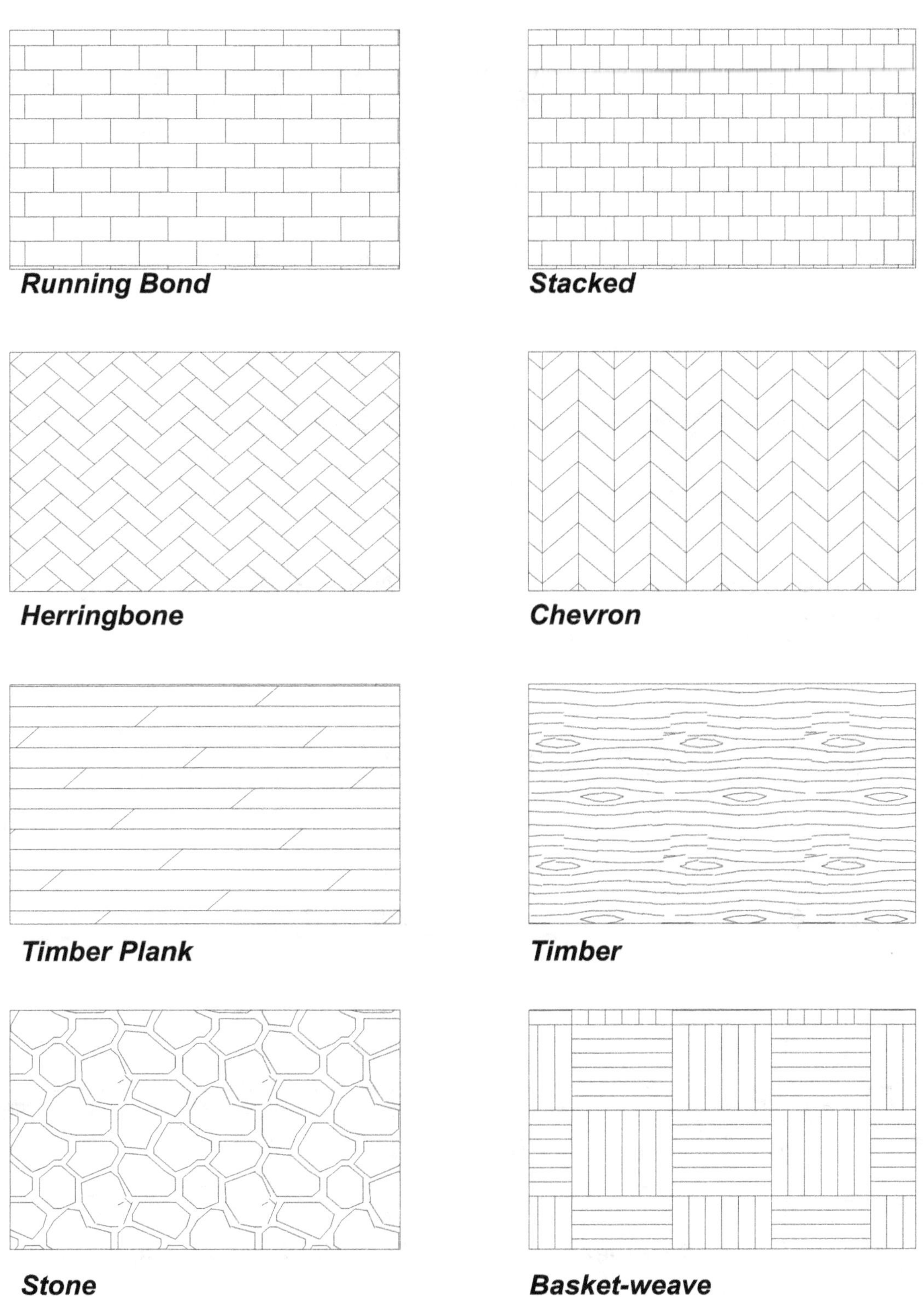

# TRANSITION EXAMPLES

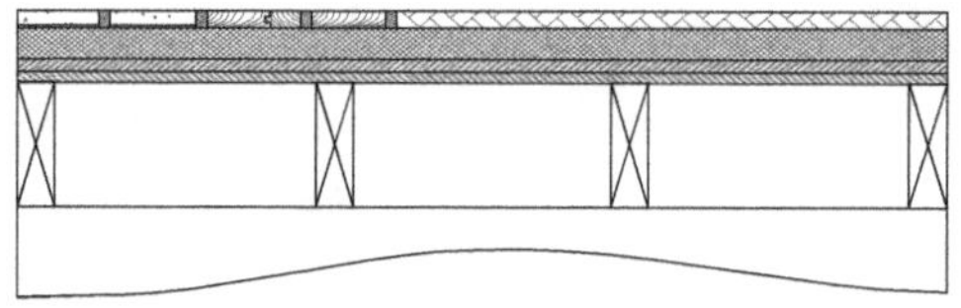

***Timber to Stone***

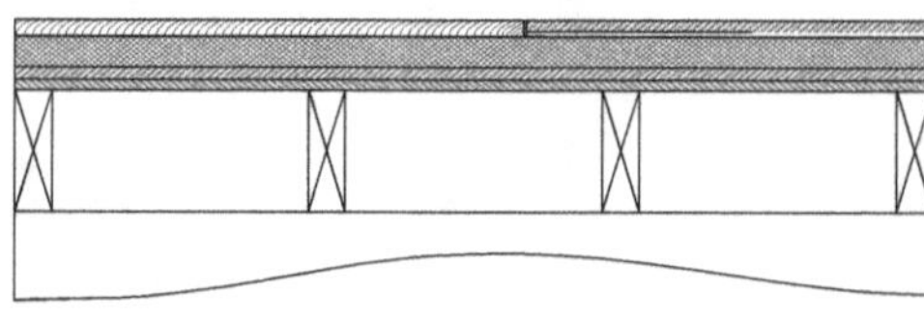

***Timber to Vinyl***

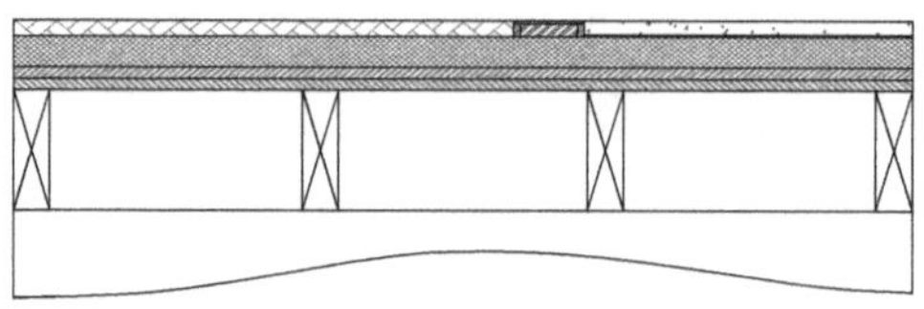

***Timber to Stone with Brass Detailing***

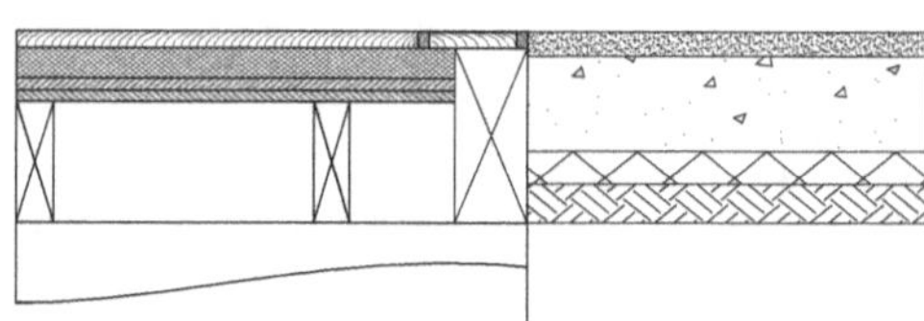

***Timber to External Paving***

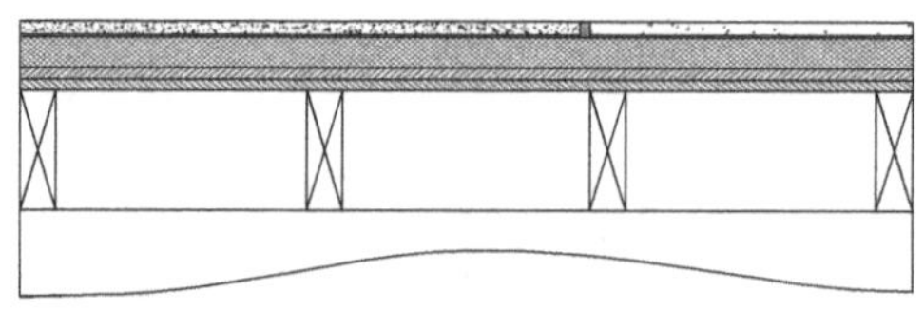

***Stone to Stone***

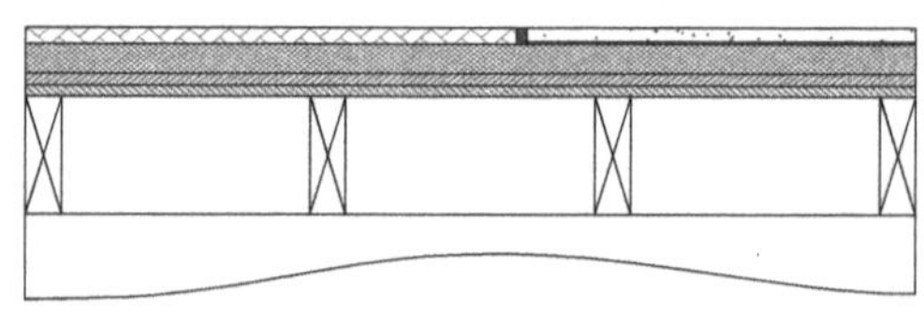

***Tile to Carpet***

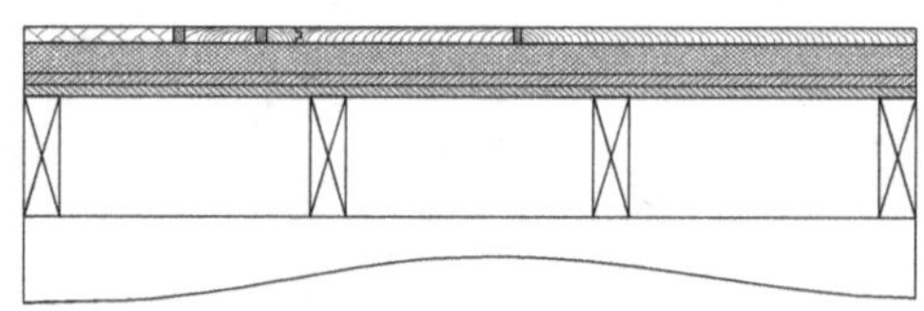

***Timber to Brass to Timber***

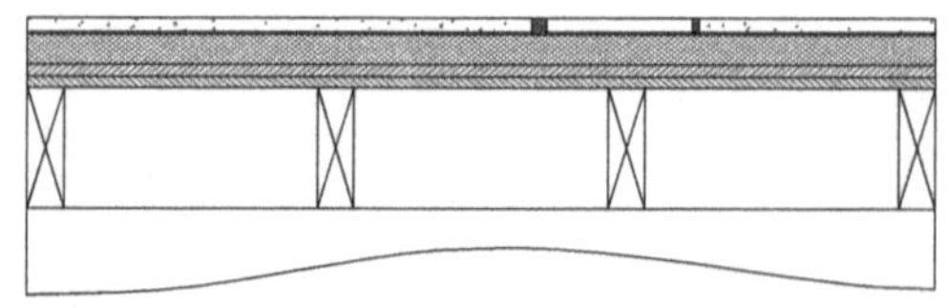

***Stone with Brass Trims***

# SHADES

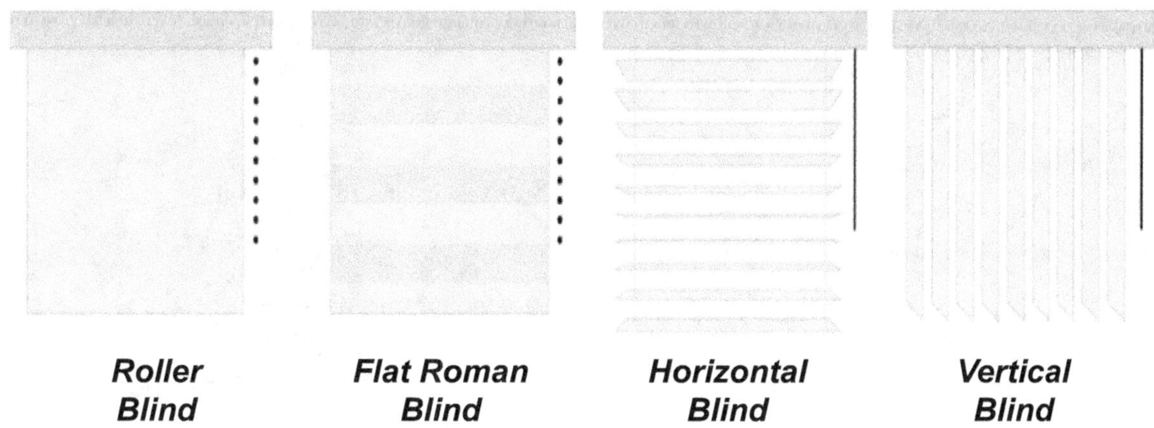

**Roller Blind**  **Flat Roman Blind**  **Horizontal Blind**  **Vertical Blind**

# DRAPERY TYPES

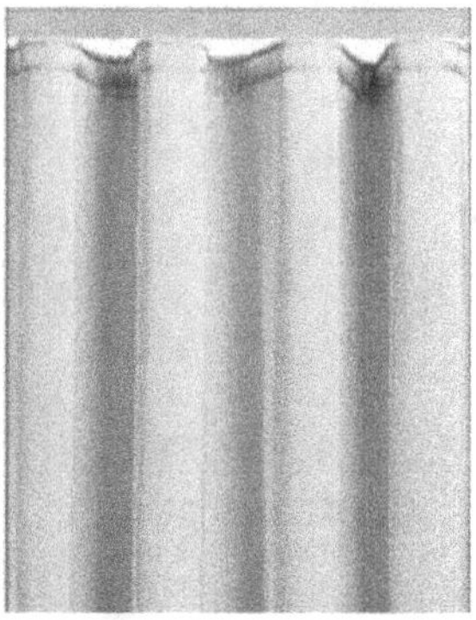

**Ripple Fold**   **Tailored Pleat** 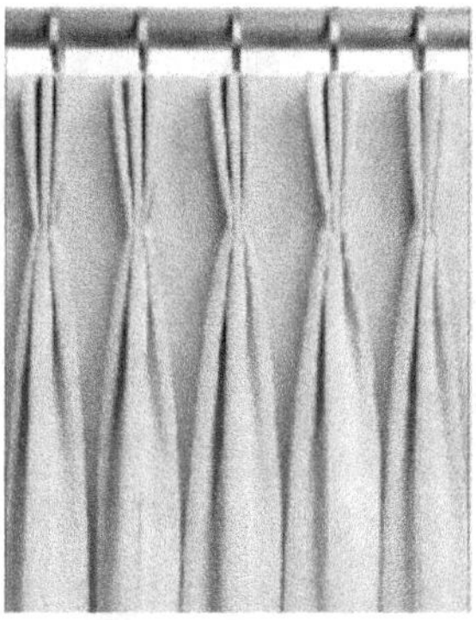  **Pinch Pleat**   **Inverted Pleat**

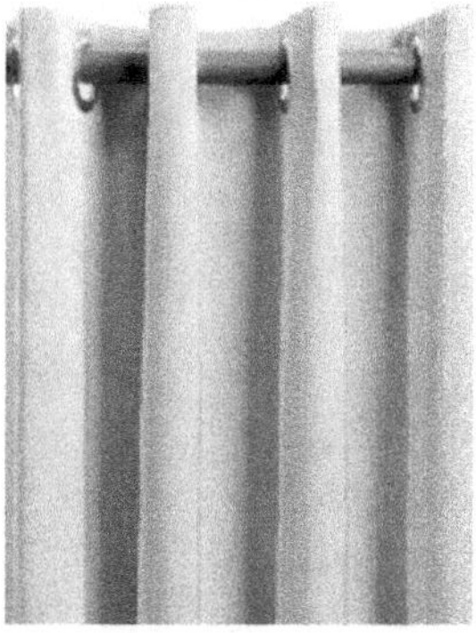

**Grommet** 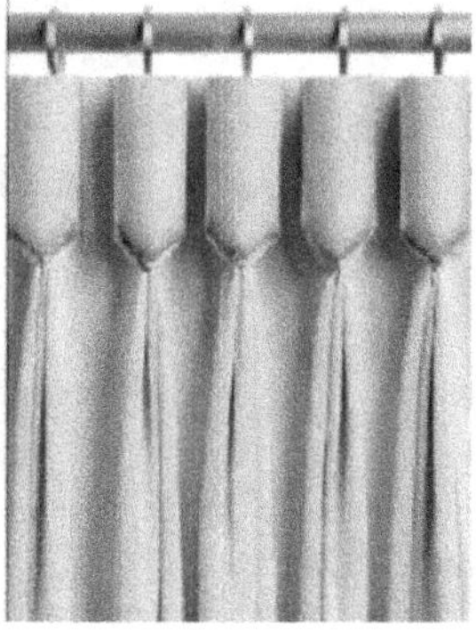  **Goblet** 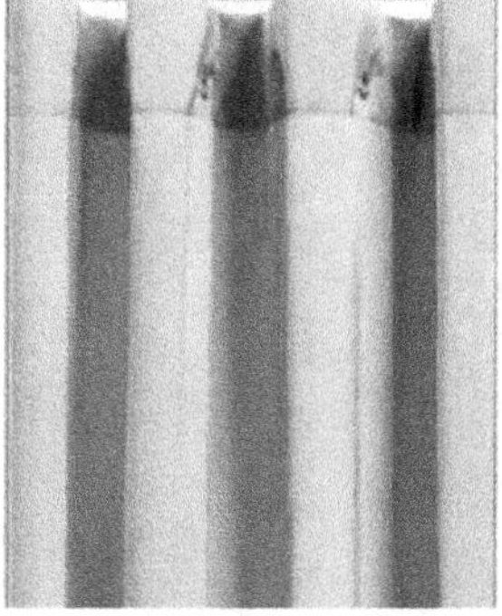  **Cubicle** 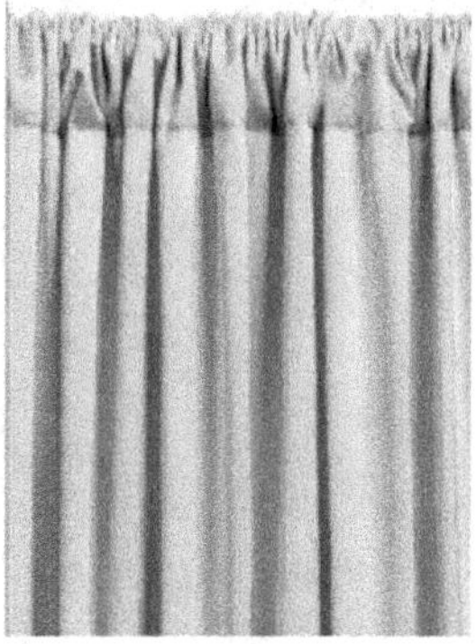  **Rod Pocket**

# HARDWOOD FLOOR CONSTRUCTION

*Chevron*

*Chantilly*

*Versailles*

*Chalosse*

*Square Basket*

*Aremberg*

*Herringbone*

*Checkerboard*

*Echelle*

# CARPET CONSTRUCTION

### Level Loop
- Loops are all the same height.
-Casual appearance, extremely durable.
-Good for family, media, and home fitness rooms.

### Multi-Level Loop
- Several different levels of loops.
- Creates a unique looking pattern.
- Casual or tailored appearance.

### Shag Pile
- Surfaces help hide footprints.
- Great texture, fun and casual appearance.
- Ideal for active families, in any room.

### Velvet / Silk
- Fine, tip sheared surface.
- Elegant style, very formal and traditional.
- Classic broadloom construction.

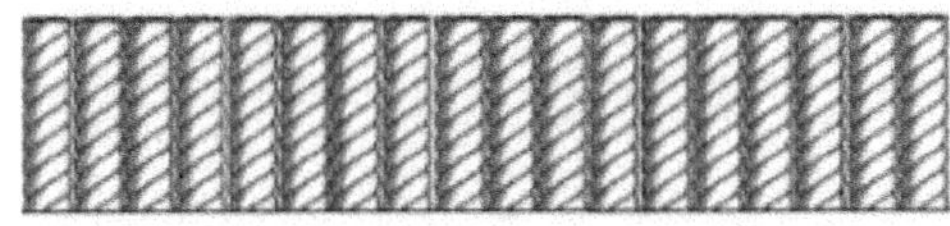

### Saxony
- Smooth, soft cut-pile surface.
- Versatile in performance.
- Works well with traditional rooms.

### Frieze
- Textured surface, with an uneven appearance.
- Extremely durable and long-wearing.
- Good for active rooms.

### Random-Sheared
- Distinctive carved appearance.
- Cut and loops give a variety of surface levels.

# TYPES OF UPHOLSTERY SEAMS

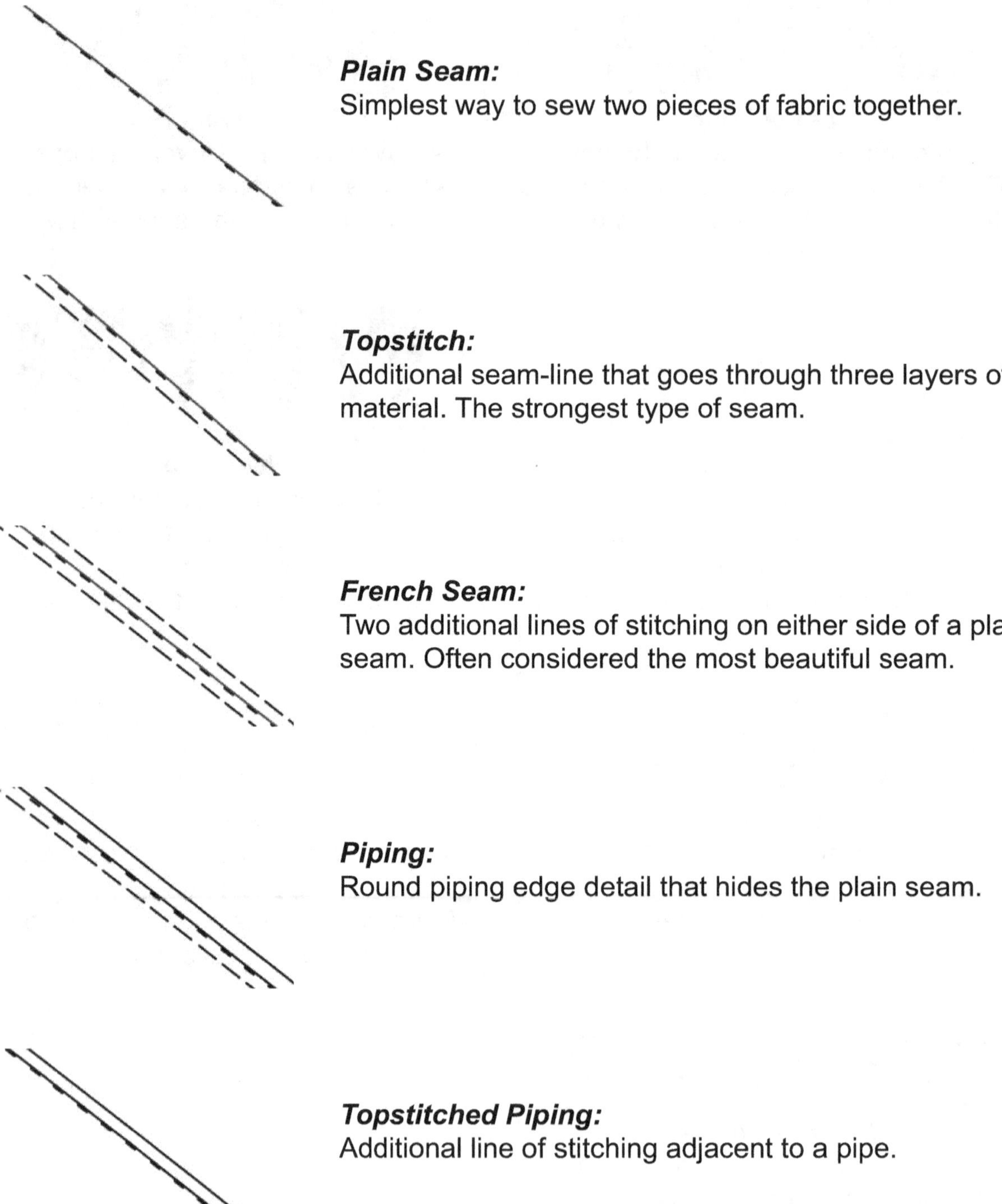

**Plain Seam:**
Simplest way to sew two pieces of fabric together.

**Topstitch:**
Additional seam-line that goes through three layers of material. The strongest type of seam.

**French Seam:**
Two additional lines of stitching on either side of a plain seam. Often considered the most beautiful seam.

**Piping:**
Round piping edge detail that hides the plain seam.

**Topstitched Piping:**
Additional line of stitching adjacent to a pipe.

**CHAPTER TEN**

# STYLES

# CONTEMPORARY

Contemporary interior design is current, modern, cutting-edge, and continuously evolving. The fluidity of contemporary interior design is particularly thrilling; what's taken into consideration in contemporary interior now will probably change over the twenty-first century. At present, contemporary interiors feature easy, unadorned spaces. Furniture tends to reveal exposed legs to create a feeling of space. Metals and glass are popular contemporary materials, and intricate details are kept to a minimum.

# MINIMALIST

The minimalist style started inside the early twentieth century and continues to spread through many components of present-day existence, interior design included. First of all, influenced via the simplicity of eastern design, minimalism works on the principle that less is more. Minimalist interiors are stripped back to their crucial elements, and space is left to make the design statement. Do not overuse colour in minimalist rooms; the idea is not to distract or detract from its simplicity. Black, white and primary hues often seem exceptional for a minimalist area.

# MID-CENTURY MODERN

Within the 1950s and '60s, a post-war America began searching to break conventional design conventions and propel its design industries into the modern-day ages. As an end result, the mid-century modern style was born. characterised by means of smooth, simple lines, bursts of blues and earthy tones, and balanced with lots of timber and rusty metals, mid-century modern is a design style with specific staying power.

# URBAN MODERN

Urban modern design derives from the cutting-edge designer lofts inside main cities like New York and Los Angeles. Taking cues from its worldly environment, urban modern is a fusion of various opposing and parallel tendencies. Minimalist modern, glamorous chic, ethnic heirlooms, and edgy experimental designs all collide in a distinctively 21st-century setting.

Larger fittings tend to be uniformly sleek with low-profile. Feel free to deliver home trailblazing modern furniture designs, accents like pillows, mirrors, console tables in urban design frequently need inventive and creative expression, add a few stylish geometric designs, or antique objects with traditional embellishment.

# INDUSTRIAL

As the name suggests, industrial design draws inspiration from a warehouse or urban loft. There's a feeling of unfinished and crude rawness in many of the details, and it's no longer surprising to see exposed brickwork, ductwork, beams and timber. A space with an industrial style might be a renovated loft from a former commercial building. High ceilings, antique woods, exposed beams and large hanging light fittings, are all details you would usually see within a space of this style. Finally, the use of large pieces of abstract artwork or photography to add a splash of colour, to an otherwise neutral colour palette stemmed from the primary materials of metal and woods.

# TRADITIONAL

A traditional design style offers classic details, luxurious furniture, and an abundance of add-ons. It's far rooted in European sensibilities. Traditional homes frequently feature dark, finished timber, rich colour palettes, and an expansion of textures and curved lines. Furnishings have intricate and ornate details and fabrics, like velvet, silk and brocade, which may include a selection of patterns and textures. There's intensity, layering and dimensionality inside most traditional designs.

# FARMHOUSE / COUNTRY

Farmhouse design is a modern-day approach to cabin-inspired interior design. Generally transitional with some conventional elements mixed in, farmhouse aesthetic must transport your creativeness to French Provence.

The furniture is characterised by distressed timber and upholstered linen. Colourwise, it is much like nautical decor with broadly speaking white and beige base hues. Orthodox regulations dictate that accent shades must be something much like turquoise or mild yellow; however, you may introduce some brighter colours for a pop of colour and definition.

# SHABBY CHIC

Shabby chic features antique elements to recreate the antique flea marketplace appearance, the furniture is characterized via their aged appearance, with distressed timber composition covered in sanded milk tones to reveal signs of wear and tear.

Decorative accents for shabby chic decor must be gentle and sumptuous, often with an affected experience, for an interior designer to convey the overall interior design to a contemporary standard. Generously introduce linen textiles for added style. Even though orthodox shabby chic colours are white, ecru and pastel, don't be afraid to use some colourful shades.

# ECLECTIC

Eclectic interiors use and adopt ideas from a range of different periods, styles and traits. Breakthrough, the guidelines of standard interior design styles, have a little fun and inject your personality into your decorating, that's what the eclectic style is all about. Nonetheless, it is crucial to maintain a feeling of balance inside your design. The very exceptional eclectic interiors are a cohesive combination of antique, new, colour, texture and patterns.

# VINTAGE

A long way from old-fashioned, vintage interiors can be highly flexible. Whether or not you're after a look that is captivating and attractive or retro and edgy, adding some key antique pieces assist you in bringing the room together. The best vintage interiors keep away from looking overly twee with the aid of maintaining clutter to a minimum. A vintage cupboard or storage unit is an appropriate manner by updating your interior in a fashionable but realistic manner. Open cabinets assist you in getting creative along with your styling, and may proudly show off any books, trinkets or antique add-ons.

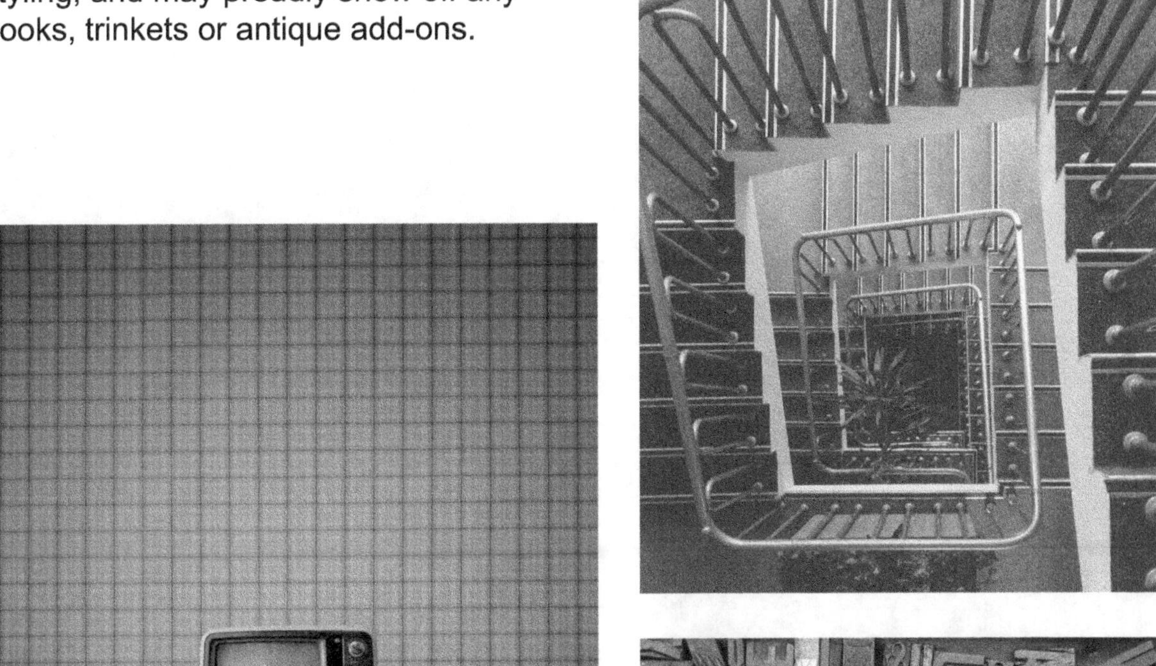

# SCANDINAVIAN

Scandinavian design will always pay homage to the simplicity of life established in Nordic nations. Scandinavian furniture design frequently feels like a piece of art, even though it is effortless and understated. There's functionality in the furniture at the side of some interesting lines, many of which have a sculptural influence.

Other common traits consist of all-white colour palettes and the incorporation of natural elements like form-pressed timber, vibrant plastics, and enamelled aluminium, metallic and huge plank flooring. If there are pops of colour, it would often come from the usage of art, natural fibre throws or furs, or a single piece of furniture. Spacious, natural lighting, minimal accessories and functional furniture characterize Scandinavian designs.

CHAPTER ELEVEN

# RESOURCES

This book only scratches the surface of what the design process encompasses. The start of a designer's education has a good resource library. Beyond the present volume, there are several publications with which the designer should be familiar. The following list is by no means exhaustive, but these texts—*some of which have served as references for this book*—expand on the topics addressed here and form the basis of a strong library.

## GENERAL REFERENCE

***Interior Design, 4th ed.***
John F. Pile; Prentice Hall, 2007

***Interior Design & Decoration, 6th ed.***
Stanley Abercrombie; Prentice Hall, 2006

***Interior Graphic and Design Standards***
S. C. Reznikoff; Whitney Library of Design, 1986

***Ppi Interior Construction & Detailing for Designers & Architects, 6th Ed.***
David Kent Ballast 1 Mar. 2019

## ESSENTIALS

***Architectural Graphics, 6th ed.***
Francis D. K. Ching; John Wiley & Sons, 2015

***The Designer and the Grid***
Lucienne Roberts and Julia Thrift; Roto-Vision, 2005

***Interior Design Illustrated, 3rd ed.***
Francis D. K. Ching and Corky Binggeli; John Wiley & Sons, 2012

***Thinking with Type: A Critical Guide for Designers, Writers, Editors, & Students, 2nd ed.***
Ellen Lupton; Princeton Architectural Press, 2010

# AREAS

***Accessible and Useable Buildings and Facilities***
International Code Council, 2009

***Archetypes in Architecture, 1st ed.***
Thomas Thiis-Evensen; Norwegian University Press, 1987

***Architectural Graphic Standards, 12th ed.***
American Institute of Architects, Dennis J. Hall eds.; John Wiley & Sons, 2016

***Art and Visual Perception***
Rudolf Arnheim; University of California Press, reprint ed., 1974

***Bathrooms: Simply Add Water, Illustrated ed.***
Terence Conran; Conran, 2006

***The Codes Guidebook for Interiors, 6th ed.***
Sharon K. Harmon and Katherine E. Kennon, eds.; Wiley, 2014

***Early American Architecture, reprint addition***
Hugh Morrison; Dover Publications, 1987

***Human Dimensions & Interior Space, revised edition***
Julius Panero and Martin Zelnik; Watson-Guptill, 1979

***Key Houses of the Twentieth Century: Plans, Sections and Elevations***
Colin Davies; Laurence King Publishing, 2006

***On the Job: Design and the American Office, 1st ed.***
Donald Albrecht and Chrysanthe B. Broikos, eds.; Princeton Architectural Press, 2000

***The Place of Houses, new edition***
Charles Moore, Gerald Allen, and Donlyn Lyndon; University of California Press, 2000

# THE FINER DETAILS

***Classic Herman Miller***
Leslie A. Piña; Schiffer Publishing, 1998

***Design Since 1945***
Peter Dormer; Thames & Hudson, 1993

***Design of the 20th Century: 25th Anniversary Edition***
Charlotte and Peter Fiell; Taschen, 2005

***Interior Design of the 20th Century: Revised and expanded edition***
Anne Massey; Thames & Hudson, 2001

***Sourcebook of Modern Furniture, 3rd ed.***
Jerryll Habegger and Joseph H. Osman; W. W. Norton, 2005

# RESOURCES

***Guide to the LEED Green Associate V4 Exam (Wiley Series in Sustainable Design)***
2nd ed Michelle Cottrell; John Wiley & Sons, 2014

***HOK Guidebook to Sustainable Design, 2nd ed.***
Sandra F. Mendler, William Odell, and Mary Ann Lazarous; John Wiley & Sons, 2005

***Sustainable Commercial Interiors, 2nd ed.***
Penny Bonda and Katie Sosnowchik; John Wiley & Sons, 2014

***Sustainable Design for Interior Environments, 2nd ed.***
Susan M. Winchip; Fairchild Books, 2011

***Sustainable Residential Interiors***
Associates III, Kari Foster, Annette Stelmack, and Debbie Hindman; John Wiley & Sons, 2006

# DIGITAL RESOURCES

## Professional Organizations

*American Institiute of Architects* www.aia.org
*American Society of Interior Designers* www.asid.org
*Association of Professional Design Firms* www.arcat.com
*British Institute of Interior Design* www.theinteriordesigninstitute.co.uk
*Chartered Society of Designers* www.csd.org.uk
*Design Institute of Australia* www.design.org.au
*Interior Design Association* www. biid.org.uk
*Interior Designer Canada* www.interiordesigncanada.org
*International Interior Design Association* www.iida.org
*Royal Architectural Institute of Canada* raic.org
*Royal Institute of British Architects* www.architecture.com
*The Society of British and International Interior Design* www.sbid.org
*U.S. Green Building Council* www.usgbc.org


## Magazines And Journals

*Abitare* (Italy) abitare.it
*Apartmento* apartamentomagazine.com
*Architect* (USA) www.architectmagazine.com
*Architectural Record* (USA) www.architecturerecord.com
*Azure* (Canada) www.azuremagazine.com
*Domus* (Italy) www.domusweb.it
*Dwell* (USA) www.dwell.com
*Elephant* elephantmag.com
*Elle Decor* (USA) www.elledecor.com
*Fast Company* fastcompany.com
*Interior Design* (USA) www.interiordesign.net
*Metropolis* (USA) www.metropolismag.com
*Surface* surfacemagazine.com
*Wallpaper** (UK) www.wallpaper.com

## Websites And Blogs

*Architizer* architizer.com
*ArchDaily* archdaily.com
*Artsy* artsy.net
*Coolhunting* coolhunting.com
*Curbed* curbed.com
*Design Boom* designboom.com
*Design Observer* designobserver.com
*Designspiration* designspiration.net
*Design*Sponge* designsponge.com

*Dezeen* dezeen.com
*iGNANT* ignant.com
*Inhabitat* inhabitat.com
*Lynda* lynda.com
*MOCO LOCO* mocoloco.com
*officeinsight* officeinsight.com
*Remodelista* remodelista.com

# SOCIAL MEDIA

*Instagram*

/ Ad_magazine
/ Ahead_awards
/ Archdigest
/ Archdigestpro
/ Christopherfarrcloth
/ Darrylclaxtoninteriors
/ Designboom
/ Dream_casa
/ Designmilk
/ Designmuseum
/ Desitecture
/ Dezeen
/ Dwellmagazine
/ Elledecor
/ Friezeartfair
/ Fourseasons
/ Houseandgarden
/ Idealhomeuk
/ Kellywearstler
/ Ralphlaurenhome
/ Riba
/ Wallpapermag

*Twitter*

@1KinDesign
@Abchome
@ArchDigest
@CAhomeanddesign
@CentsantionalGrl
@Contractmag
@ElleDecor
@Freshome
@Homeadore
@HomesandGardens
@Homedesigning
@HomeTrendsMag
@HouseBeautiful
@Interiordesign
@IIDA_HQ
@Lonnymag
@Luxemag
@Materialgirls
@Onekindesign
@StyleatHome

# SOFTWARE

## CAD AND MODELING

**ArchiCAD** archicad.com
**AutoCAD** autodesk.com
**Blender** blender.org
**Cinema 4D** maxon.net
**form•Z** formz.com
**Revit** autodesk.com
**Rhinoceros** rhino3d.com
**SketchUp** sketchup.com
**Vectorworks** nemetschek.net

## ONLINE MODELING

**Onshape** onshape.com
**SketchUp** sketchup.com
**Tinkercad** tinkercad.com

## RENDERING

**Corona** corona-renderer.com
**Maxwell** maxwellrender.com
**Octane** home.otoy.com
**Unity** unity3d.com
**V-Ray** chaosgroup.com

# MANUALS

**Metric Handbook: Planning and Design Data, 6th ed.**
Pamela Buxton 15 Jan 2018

**Architect's Pocket Book (Routledge Pocket Books), 5th ed.**
Jonathan Hetreed, Ann Ross, et al. 15 Apr 2017

**Building Regulations Pocket Book (Routledge Pocket Books)**
Ray Tricker (Author), Samantha Alford (Author) 16 Feb. 2018

# INDUSTRY ASSOCIATIONS

**Americans with Disabilities Act** ada.gov
**Architectural Woodwork Association** awinet.org
**Building Stone Institute** buildingstoneinstitute.org
**Carpet and Rug Institute** carpet-rug.org
**Design at the Design Museum** designmuseum.org/design
**National Wood Flooring Association** woodfloors.org
**Whole Building Design Guide** wbdg.org

# Index

# CREDITS

Photographic resources are mentioned alongside the photographs; uncredited photographs, all renderings and drawings are by the author.

Every attempt has been made to cite all resources; if a reference has been missed, please contact the author for correction in subsequent editions.

# DISCLAIMER

This publication is designed to provide accurate and authoritative information in regard to the subject matter covered. It is sold with the understanding that the author is not held responsible for any outdated information in the future. If professional advice or other expert assistance is required, the services of a competent professional should be sought. All photographs, documents, and forms are proprietary to the organization, design firm, designer, or author. None of the figures in this text may be reproduced without the expressed written permission of the appropriate copyright holder.

# COPYRIGHT

# NOTES

# NOTES

# NOTES

# NOTES

# ABOUT THE AUTHOR

## **Darryl Claxton**

DARRYLCLAXTONINTERIORS

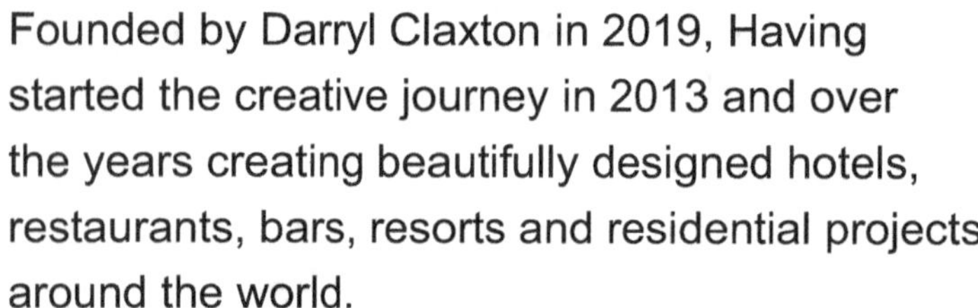

Founded by Darryl Claxton in 2019, Having started the creative journey in 2013 and over the years creating beautifully designed hotels, restaurants, bars, resorts and residential projects around the world.

At the heart of DARRYLCLAXTONINTERIORS is a commitment to the individual and their experience of an interior. Through the careful study of a project's brief, context and a client's lifestyle, a dedication to functionality and a love of combining different materials, textures and styles, hand-crafting environments that enable the client to develop personal and long-lasting relationships with their interiors.

www.dclaxtoninteriors.com

www.ingramcontent.com/pod-product-compliance
Lightning Source LLC
Chambersburg PA
CBHW080259030726
47593CB00009B/2545